a Ros
1963

A Choice of de la Mare's Verse

Verse by Walter de la Mare

*

COLLECTED POEMS
COLLECTED RHYMES AND VERSES
SELECTED POEMS
SONGS OF CHILDHOOD
PEACOCK PIE
BELLS AND GRASS
O LOVELY ENGLAND
WINGED CHARIOT
INWARD COMPANION
THE BURNING-GLASS
THE TRAVELLER
TIME PASSES
STUFF AND NONSENSE
THE WINNOWING DREAM

A CHOICE OF
DE LA MARE'S VERSE

Selected
with an introduction
by
W. H. AUDEN

FABER AND FABER
24 Russell Square
London

First published in mcmlxiii
by Faber and Faber Limited
24 Russell Square London W.C.1
Printed in Great Britain by
R. MacLehose and Company Limited
The University Press Glasgow

Contents

8

III

IV

V

VIII

IX

Introduction

As an introduction to that best of all anthologies for the young, *Come Hither,* Mr de la Mare wrote a parable. A schoolboy named Simon has heard from his mother about a wonderful place of 'trees, waters, green pastures, rare birds and flowers' called East Dene. Setting out one morning to look for it, he comes to an old stone house in a hollow called Thrae, and makes the acquaintance of its owner, Miss Taroone. When he asks her about East Dene, she gives him a strange look but does not answer. She tells him, however, that Thrae is not her only house, and speaks of Sure Vine 'as a family mansion, very ancient and magnificent'. She also tells him about a great traveller, Mr Nahum.

'I could not at first make head or tail of Mr Nahum. Even now I am uncertain whether he was Miss Taroone's brother or her nephew or a cousin many times removed; or whether perhaps she was really and truly Mrs Taroone and he her only son; or she still Miss Taroone and he an adopted one. I am not sure whether she had much love for him, though she appeared to speak of him with pride. What I do know is that Miss Taroone had nurtured him from his cradle and had taught him all the knowledge that was not already his by right of birth. . . . Strangely enough, by the looks on her face and the tones of her voice, Mr Taroone was inclined to mock a little at Mr Nahum because of his restlessness. She didn't seem to approve of his leaving her so much — though she herself had come from Sure Vine.'

The names are easy to translate and the general drift of

the parable is clear. Because of his peculiar position as a traveller in search of a joy which he has yet to find and can only imagine in terms of an innocent happiness which is no longer his, every man, whether as a writer or a reader of poetry, demands two things which, though not absolutely incompatible with each other, are not easy to reconcile completely. On the one hand, we want a poem to be a beautiful object, a verbal Garden of Eden which, by its formal perfection, keeps alive in us the hope that there exists a state of joy without evil or suffering which it can and should be our destiny to attain. At the same time, we look to a poem for some kind of illumination about our present wandering condition, since, without self-insight and knowledge of the world, we must err blindly with little chance of realizing our hope. We expect a poem to tell us some home truth, however minor, and, as we know, most home truths are neither pretty nor pleasant. One might say that, in every poet, there dwells an Ariel, who sings, and a Prospero, who comprehends, but in any particular poem, sometimes even in the whole work of a particular poet, one of the partners plays a greater role than the other. Thus Campion, one of de la Mare's favourite poets, is an example of an Ariel-dominated poet in whose work verbal beauty is *almost* everything, and what is said matters very little. In Wordsworth's *The Prelude*, on the other hand, Prospero dominates and Ariel contributes very little; it might *almost* have been written in prose.

Though the role of Prospero in de la Mare's poetry is much greater than one may realize on a first reading, it would not be unfair, I think, to call him an Ariel-dominated poet. Certainly, his most obvious virtues, those which no reader can fail to see immediately, are verbal and formal, the delicacy of his metrical fingering and the graceful architecture of his stanzas. Neither in his technique nor his sensibility, does he show any trace of influences other than English, either continental, like Eliot and Pound, or Classical, like Bridges. The poets from whom he seems to have learned most are the Elizabethan song-writers, Christina Rossetti and, I would rashly guess, Thomas Hardy. Like Christina Rossetti, he is a master of trisyllabic substitution and foot inversion; the reader's ear is continually excited by rhythmical variations without ever losing a sense of the underlying pattern. In the predominantly anapaestic movement of the following stanza, for example, how surprising and yet convincing is the sudden shift to a trochaic movement in the fifth line and to a spondaic in the sixth.

> Wicket out into the dark
>> That swings but one way;
> Infinite hush in an ocean of silence
>> Aeons away —
> *Thou* forsaken! — even thou! —
>> The dread good-bye;
> The abandoned, the thronged, the watched, the unshared —
>> Awaiting me — I!

Like Hardy, he is a great inventor of stanzas and in command of every effect which can be obtained from contrasts between lines of different lengths, lines with masculine endings and lines with feminine endings, rhymed and unrhymed lines.

> 'Tis strange to see young children
> In such a wintry house;
> Like rabbits on the frozen snow
> Their tell-tale foot-prints go;

Their laughter rings like timbrels
'Neath evening ominous.

* * *

He drew each pure heart with his skill;
With his beauty,
And his azure,
And his topaz,
Gold for pleasure,
And his locks wet with the dew of April.

* * *

Once gay, now sad; remote — and dear;
Why turn away in doubt and fear?
I search again your grieved self-pitying face;
Kindness sits clouded there. But, love? No, not a trace.

Many poets have some idiosyncrasy or tic of style which
can madden the reader if he finds their work basically
unsympathetic, but which, if he likes it, becomes endear-
ing like the foibles of an old friend. Hardy's fondness for
compound and latinate words is one example, de la
Mare's habit of subject-verb inversion another

Leans now the fair willow, dreaming
Amid her locks of green.

In his later work such inversions become much rarer.
One can observe also a change in his diction. Though
this continues to come from what one might call the
'beautiful' end of the verbal spectrum — he never, like
Yeats and Eliot uses a coarse or brutal word, and seldom a
slang colloquialism — a chronological study of his poems
shows a steady, patient and successful endeavour to elim-
inate the overly arty diction which was a vice of his Pre-
Raphaelite forebears, and to develop a style which, without ceasing to be lyrical, has the directness of ordinary

16

speech. What a distance, there is, for example, between these two extracts, one from an early poem, one from a late.

> Slowly, silently, now the moon
> Walks the night in her silver shoon;
> This way, and that, she peers, and sees
> Silver fruit upon silver trees;
> One by one the casements catch
> Her beams beneath the silvery thatch;

* * *

> What, do you suppose, we're in this world for, sweet heart?
> What — in this haunted, crazy, beautiful cage —
> *Keeps* so many, like ourselves, poor pining human creatures,
> As if from some assured, yet golden heritage?
> Keeps us lamenting beneath all our happy laughter,
> Silence, dreams, hope for what may *not* come after,
> While life wastes and withers, as it has for mortals,
> > Age on to age, on to age.

His late long poem, *Winged Chariot,* is a surprising performance. He still writes as a lyric poet, not as an epic or dramatic, and it is better read, perhaps, like *In Memoriam,* as a series of lyrics with a metre and theme in common, but readers who are only familiar with his early poetry will find something they would never have predicted, a talent for metaphysical wit.

> The dwindling candle with her pensive light
> Metes out the leaden watches of the night.
> And, in that service, from herself takes flight.

* * *

> Fate was appalled. Her See-Saw would not stir.
> Man sat dead-centre and grimaced at her.
> Her prizes? None could shine where none could err;
> So every dunce was a philosopher.

* * *

Cowed by the spectre for which 'no man waits',
Obsequious hirelings of the witless Fates,
Time pins down ev'n Dictators to their 'dates'.

De la Mare wrote many poems with an audience of
children specifically in mind, and, in his collected works,
these have been published in a volume by themselves.
This has a practical convenience, but it must never be
forgotten that, while there are some good poems which
are only for adults, because they pre-suppose adult experience in their readers, there are no good poems which are
only for children. Human beings are blessed with the
power to remember; consequently, to grow old means for
us, not to discard but to accumulate; in every old man,
there still lives a child, an adolescent, a young man and a
middle-aged one. It is commonly believed that childern
are, by nature, more imaginative than adults, but this is
questionable. It is probably the case only in cultures like
our own which put a higher social and economic value
upon practical and abstract thinking than upon wonder
and images; in a culture which put a high value on
imagination and a low one on logic, children might well
appear to be more rational than adults, for a child is not,
by nature, more *anything*. In all cultures, however, there is
one constant difference between children and adults,
namely, that, for the former, learning their native tongue
is itself one of the most important experiences in their lives,
while, for the latter, language has become an instrument
for interpreting and communicating experience; to re-
capture the sense of language as experience, an adult has
to visit a foreign country.

What the child, and the child-in-the-adult, most enjoys
in poetry, therefore, is the manipulation of language for its

18

own sake, the sound and rhythm of words. There is a deplorable tendency in the United States, which I hope and pray has not spread to the United Kingdom, to think that books for children should use a very limited vocabulary, and that verses for them should be written in the simplest and most obvious metres. This is utter nonsense. The surest sign that a child has a feeling for language is that he talks like an affected adult and always uses a polysyllabic word when a monosyllabic one would do.

As a revelation of the wonders of the English Language, de la Mare's poems for children are unrivalled. (The only ones which do not seem to me quite to come off are those in which he tries to be humorous. A gift, like Hilaire Belloc's for the comic-satiric is not his; he lacks, perhaps, both the worldliness and the cruelty which the genre calls for.) They include what, for the adult, are among his greatest 'pure' lyrics, e.g. *Old Shellover* and *The Song of the Mad Prince*, and their rhythms are as subtle as they are varied. Like all good poems, of course, they do more than train the ear. They also teach sensory attention and courage. Unlike a lot of second-rate verse for children, de la Mare's descriptions of birds, beasts, and natural phenomena are always sharp and accurate, and he never prettifies experience or attempts to conceal from the young that terror and nightmare are as essential characteristics of human existence as love and sweet dreams. There is another respect in which, as all writers of good books for them know, children differ from grown-ups; they have a far greater tolerance for didactic instruction, whether in facts or morals. As Chesterton observed:

'The child does not know that men are not only bad from good motives, but also often good from bad motives. Therefore the

19

child has a hearty, unspoiled, and insatiable appetite for mere morality, for the mere difference between a good little girl and a bad little girl.'

Without ever being tiresome, de la Mare is not afraid to instruct the young. What could be more practically useful than his mnemonic rhyme *Stars*, or more educative, morally as well as musically, than *Hi!*?

> Hi! handsome hunting man
> Fire your little gun.
> Bang! Now the animal
> Is dead and dumb and done.
> Nevermore to peep again, creep again, leap again,
> Eat or sleep or drink again, Oh, what fun!

In considering the work of any poet, it is always easier and safer to discuss the role of Ariel than that of Prospero. There is only one Ariel to a language, but there are as many Prosperos as there are poets. We can describe what one poet does with the language and compare it with what another poet has done, but we cannot compare the perspective on life of any poet with that of any other because each is unique. That is why poets themselves hate being asked what their poems 'mean' because, in order to answer such a question, they would have to know themselves which, as Thoreau said, is as impossible as seeing oneself from the back without turning one's head. Every poet will second de la Mare's statement in his prefatory note to O *Lovely England*.

> 'What a writer has to say *about* his "poems" and their subterranean waters, is often dangerous, and may be even scientifically innaccurate. Verbal and metrical craftsmanship is another matter. . . .'

But, as readers of poetry, we can no more help asking, 'What is it about this poem, aside from its formal beauties or defects, which makes it sympathetic or unsympathetic to me?', than we can help trying to analyse the qualities of a fellow human being to whom, positively or negatively, we respond. What we 'see' in a person or a poem may be quite wrong and is certainly only part of the truth but, if we talk about either, we can only say what we see.

Though all poetry is, ultimately, about human nature, many poems do not look at man directly, but at what he is not, the non-human part of creation which, by convention, we call 'Nature' (though it may also contain human arte-facts). In the work of certain poets, and de la Mare is one of them, the landscape speaks. His personal landscape is derived from two sources. Firstly, there is the countryside of pre-industrial England, so beautiful in an unspectacular way, and so kindly in climate. (Perhaps, having never suffered from bronchitis, I am biased.) The setting of one poem is a railway-junction, in another the lyric 'I' rides a bus, there are a few references to water-mills, but otherwise there is no machinery and no modern building.

As the work of some of the Georgian poets bears witness, the danger of the English landscape as a poetic ingredient is that its gentleness can tempt those who love it into writing genteely. De la Mare was protected from this, firstly by his conviction that what our senses perceive of the world about us is not all there is to know, and, secondly, by his sense of the powers of evil. This does not mean that he is a Buddhist who regards the sensory world as illusion, or that he would call what we normally are blind to super-natural. His view, I take it, is that our eyes and ears do not lie to us, but do not, perhaps cannot, tell us the whole truth, and that those who deny this, end up by actually narrowing their vision.

'What is called realism is usually a record of life at a low pitch and ebb viewed in the sunless light of day — so often a drab waste of gray and white, and an east wind blowing.'

What we would see, if our senses and imagination were keener, might be more beautiful than anything we have known.

'It seemed to be a house which might at any moment vanish before your eyes, showing itself to be but the outer shell or hiding place of an abode still more enchanting. . . . If you ever sat and watched a Transformation Scene in a pantomime, did you suppose, just before the harlequin slapped with his wand on what looked like a plain brick-and-mortar wall, that it would instantly after dissolve into a radiant coloured scene of trees and fountains and hidden beings — growing lovelier in their own showing as the splendour spread and their haunts were revealed? Well, so at times I used to feel in Thrae.'

On the other hand, the most beautiful object might turn out to be hiding something neither beautiful nor friendly.

> Masked by that brilliant weed's deceitful green,
> No glint of the dark water can be seen
> Which, festering, slumbers, with this scum for screen.
>
> It is as though a face, as false as fair,
> Dared not, by smiling, show the evil there.

* * *

> Darkness had fallen. I opened the door:
> And lo, a stranger in the empty room —
> A marvel of moonlight upon wall and floor. . . .
> The quiet of mercy? Or the hush of doom?

Nor, whatever it might turn out to be, can we be certain that, were we mortals to be confronted by the truth, we could endure it.

> Might that secret, if divulged, all we value most bewray!
>   Make a dream of our real,
>   A night of our day. . . .

22

The other element, more romantic and more disturbing, in the de la Mare landscape is partly derived from Grimm's Maerchen and similar folk-tales, and partly from dreams.

> Still and blanched and cold and lone
> The icy hills far off from me
> With frosty ulys overgrown
> Stand in their sculptured secrecy.
>
> No path of theirs the chamois fleet
> Treads with a nostril to the wind;
> O'er their ice-marbled glaciers beat
> No wings of eagles to my mind.

Again, the overestimation of dreams and the subjective life shown by some of the lesser Romantic poets, can become boring, for most people are even less original in their dreaming than in their waking life; their dreams are more monotonous than their thoughts and, oddly enough, more literary. Fortunately, de la Mare, as those who have read *Behold This Dreamer* will have learned, was one of those uncommon persons whose dreams are really original. Like Blake, he possessed the rare gift of having visions while awake. (Mescaline and lysergic acid can, it now seems, confer it on us dullards.) He tells, for instance, how once, after dreaming that the Flora of Primavera herself was at that moment passing beneath his bedroom window, he woke up, went to the window, and there, sure enough, she was in the street.

> 'She sat, uplifted, etherally lovely, surrounded by her attendant nymphs and *amorini*, and crowned and wreathed with flowers. It was with ropes of flowers, also, that her nymphs were drawing slowly on her low flat Car on its wide clumsy wooden wheels, like gigantic cotton-reels.

'Every artist' said Santayana, ' is a moralist though he needn't preach,' and de la Mare is one who doesn't. His

23

poems are neither satirical nor occasional; indeed, I cannot recall coming across in his work a single Proper Name, whether of a person or a place, which one could identify as a real historical name. Nor, though he is a lyric, not a dramatic, poet, are his poems 'personal' in the sense of being self-confessions; the *I* in them is never identical with the Mr de la Mare one might have met at dinner, and none are of the kind which excite the curiosity of a biographer. Nevertheless, implicit in all his poetry are certain notions of what constitutes the Good Life. Goodness, they seem to say, is rooted in wonder, awe, and reverence for the beauty and strangeness of creation. Wonder itself is not goodness — de la Mare is not an aesthete — but it is the only, or the most favourable, soil in which goodness can grow. Those who lose the capacity for wonder may become clever but not intelligent, they may lead moral lives themselves, but they will become insensitive and moralistic towards others. A sense of wonder is not something we have to learn, for we are born with it; unfortunately, we are also born with an aggressive lust for power which finds its satisfaction in the enslavement and destruction of others. We are, or in the course of our history we have become, predatory animals like the mousing cat and the spotted flycatcher. This lust for power, which, if we surrender completely to it, can turn us into monsters like Seaton's Aunt, is immanent in every child.

> Lovely as Eros, and half-naked too,
> He heaped dried beach-drift, kindled it, and, lo!
> A furious furnace roared, the sea-winds blew. . .
> Vengeance divine! And death to every foe!

Young god! and not ev'n Nature eyed askance
The fire doomed Empire of a myriad ants.

It is only with the help of wonder, then, that we can
develop a virtue which we are certainly not born with,
compassion, not to be confused with its conceit-created
counterfeit, pity. Only from wonder, too, can we learn a
style of behaviour and speech which is no less precious in
art than in life; for want of a better word we call it
good-manners or breeding, though it has little to do with
ancestry, school or income. To be well-bred means to
have respect for the solitude of others, whether they be
mere acquaintances or, and this is much more difficult,
persons we love; to be ill-bred is to importune attention
and intimacy, to come too close, to ask indiscreet questions
and make indiscreet revelations, to lecture, to bore.

Making a selection from the work of any poet one
admires is a job which cannot be done satisfactorily
because one is always conscious that everything he wrote,
even the second best, should be read. De la Mare has, in
my opinion, been very shabbily treated by anthologists; in
their selections, most have been content to copy each other,
and few have included poems he wrote after 1920. This
is a gross injustice to a poet who continued to mature,
both in technique and wisdom, till the day of his death.

W. H. AUDEN

I

The Enchanted Hill

From height of noon, remote and still,
The sun shines on the empty hill.
No mist, no wind, above, below;
No living thing strays to and fro.
No bird replies to bird on high,
Cleaving the skies with echoing cry.
Like dreaming water, green and wan,
Glassing the snow of mantling swan,
Like a clear jewel encharactered
With secret symbol of line and word,
Asheen, unruffled, slumbrous, still,
The sunlight streams on the empty hill.

But soon as Night's dark shadows ride
Across its shrouded Eastern side,
When at her kindling, clear and full,
Star beyond star stands visible;
Then course pale phantoms, fleet-foot deer
Lap of its waters icy clear.
Mounts the large moon, and pours her beams
On bright-fish-flashing, singing streams.
Voices re-echo. Coursing by,
Horsemen, like clouds, wheel silently.
Glide then from out their pitch-black lair
Beneath the dark's ensilvered arch,
Witches becowled into the air;
And iron pine and emerald larch,
Tents of delight for ravished bird,
Are by loud music thrilled and stirred.

Winging the light, with silver feet,
Beneath their bowers of fragrance met,
In dells of rose and meadowsweet,
In mazy dance the fairies flit;
While drives his share the Ploughman high
Athwart the daisy-powdered sky:
Till far away, in thickening dew,
Piercing the Eastern shadows through,
Rilling in crystal clear and still,
Light 'gins to tremble on the hill.
And like a mist on faint winds borne,
Silent, forlorn, wells up the morn.
Then the broad sun with burning beams
Steeps slope and peak and gilded streams.
Then no foot stirs; the brake shakes not;
Soundless and wet in its green grot
As if asleep, the leaf hangs limp;
The white dews drip untrembling down,
From bough to bough, orblike, unblown;
And in strange quiet, shimmering and still,
Morning enshrines the empty hill.

The Risen Sun

I lay a while, exulting in its light,
My Druid heart drenched through with awe and praise;
Then into darkness turned a dazzled sight,
      That dared not meet its gaze.

Dawn

Near, far, unearthly, break the birds
From spectral bush and tree,
Into a strange and drowsy praise,
The flush of dawn to see.

Old ashen rooks, on ragged wing,
And heads with sidling eye,
Sweep in the silvery heights of daybreak,
Silent through the sky.

The restless robin — like a brook
Tinkling in frozen snow —
Shakes his clear, sudden, piercing bells,
Flits elf-like to and fro.

Cock to cock yells, the enormous earth
Lies like a dream outspread
Under the canopy of space,
Stretched infinite overhead.

Light on the wool-fleeced ewes pours in;
Meek-faced they snuff the air;
The glint-horned oxen sit agaze;
The east burns orient-fair.

The milk-white mists of night wreathe up
From meadows greenly grey —
Their every blade of grass ablaze
With dewdrops drenched in day.

Five Eyes

In Hans' old Mill his three black cats
Watch his bins for the thieving rats.
Whisker and claw, they crouch in the night,
Their five eyes smouldering green and bright:
Squeaks from the flour sacks, squeaks from where
The cold wind stirs on the empty stair,
Squeaking and scampering, everywhere.
Then down they pounce, now in, now out,
At whisking tail, and sniffing snout;

While lean old Hans he snores away
Till peep of light at break of day;
Then up he climbs to his creaking mill,
Out come his cats all grey with meal —
Jekkel, and Jessup, and one-eyed Jill.

'I Dream of a Place'

I dream of a place where I long to live always:
Green hills, shallow sand dunes, and nearing the sea;

The house is of stone; there are twelve lattice windows,
And a door, with a keyhole — though lost is the key.

Thick-thatched is the roof; it has low, white-washed chimneys,
Where doves preen their wings, and coo, *Please*, love: love *me*!

There martins are flitting; the sun shines; the moon shines;
Drifts of bright flowers are adrone with the bee;

And a wonderful music of bird-song at daybreak
Wells up from the bosom of every tree.

A brook of clear water encircles the garden,
With kingcups, and cress, and the white *fleur de lys* —

Moorhens and dabchicks; the wild duck at evening
Wing away to the sun, in the shape of a V;

And the night shows the stars, shining in at the windows,
Brings nearer the far-away sigh of the sea.

Oh, the quiet, the green of the grass, the grey willows,
The light, and the shine, and the air sweet and free! —

That dream of a place where I long to live always:
Low hills, shallow sand dunes — at peace there to be!

Somewhere

Would you tell me the way to Somewhere?
Somewhere, Somewhere,
I have heard of a place called Somewhere —
But know not where it can be.
It makes no difference,
Whether or not
I go in dreams
Or trudge on foot:
Could you tell me the way to Somewhere,
The Somewhere meant for me?

There's a little old house in Somewhere —
        Somewhere, Somewhere,
A queer little house, with a Cat and a Mouse —
        Just room enough for three.
                A kitchen, a larder,
                A bin for bread,
                A string of candles,
                Or stars instead,
                A table, a chair,
                And a four-post bed —
There's room for us all in Somewhere,
        For the Cat and the Mouse and Me.

Puss is called *Skimme* in Somewhere,
        In *Somewhere, Somewhere;*
        Miaou, miaou, in Somewhere,
        S — K — I — M — M — E.

                Miss Mouse is scarcely
                One inch tall,
                So *she* never needed
                A name at all;
                And though you call,
                And call, and call,
                There squeaks no answer,
                Great or small —
Though her tail is a sight times longer
        Than this is likely to be : —

                FOR
I want to be *off* to Somewhere,
To far, lone, lovely Somewhere,
No matter where Somewhere be.

akes no difference
ether or not
in sleep
trudge on foot,
this time to-morrow
w far I've got,
nmer or Winter,
Cold, or hot,
Where, or When,
Or Why, or What —
Please, tell me the way to Somewhere —
Somewhere, Somewhere ;
Somewhere, Somewhere, Somewhere, SOMEWHERE —
The Somewhere meant for me !

The Hunt

Tallyho! Tallyho! —
Echo faints far astray,
On the still, misty air,
And the Hunt is away !

Horsemen and hounds
Stream over the hill ;
And, brush well behind him,
Pelts with a will
Old Reynard the Fox —
As in conscience he may,
For hot at his heels
Sweep Trim, Trap and Tray ;
Chestnut, and black,
And flea-bitten grey.
But the Crafty One knows
Every inch of the way !

Thicket and spinney,
Gully and dell,
Where the stream runs deep,
And the otters dwell —
Hemlock, garlic,
Bog asphodel —
He'll lead them a dance,
Though they ride like hell.
And — wily old animal,
Cunning as they ! —
He'll live — to go hunting —
Another fine day.

Sheep

Early sunbeams shafting the beech-boles,
  An old oak fence, and in pasture deep —
Dark, and shapeless, dotting the shadows —
  A grazing and motionless flock of sheep;

So strangely still as they munched the grasses
  That I, up aloft on my 'bus, alone,
At gaze from its glass on the shimmering highway,
  Cried on myself : — 'Not sheep ! They are stone !' —

Sarsen outcrops shelved by the glaciers?
  An aeon of darkness, ice and snow?
Beings bewitched out of far-away folk-tales?
  Prodigies such as dreams can show?

The mind — that old mole — has its hidden earthworks:
  Blake's greybeard into a thistle turned ;
And, in his childhood, flocking angels
  In sun-wild foliage gleamed and burned.

Illusions . . . Yet — as my 'bus lurched onward,
  Beech trees, park-land and woodland gone,
It was not sheep in my memory lingered
  But, strangely indwelling, those shapes of stone.

34

Martins

'*Chelidon urbica urbica!*'
I cried on the little bird,
Meticulously enunciating each syllable of each word;
   '*Chelidon urbica urbica!*'
   Listen to me, I plead!
There are swallows all snug in the hayloft,
I have all that your nestlings can need —
Shadow and sunshine and sweet shallow water —
Come, build in my eaves, and breed!

Fly high, my love! My love, fly low!
I watched the sweet pretty creatures go —
Floating, skimming, and wheeling so
Swiftly and softly — like flakes of snow,
'Gainst the dark of the cedar-boughs, to and fro: . . .
      But no!
      But no!
   '*Chelidon urbica urbica!*'
   None paid me the faintest heed.

A Riddle

The mild noon air of Spring again
Lapped shimmering in that sea-lulled lane.
Hazel was budding; wan as snow
The leafless blackthorn was a-blow.

A chaffinch clankt, a robin woke
An eerie stave in the leafless oak.
Green mocked at green; lichen and moss
The rain-worn slate did softly emboss.

35

From out her winter lair, at sigh
Of the warm South wind, a butterfly
Stepped, quaffed her honey; on painted fan
Her labyrinthine flight began.

Wondrously solemn, golden and fair,
The high sun's rays beat everywhere;
Yea, touched my cheek and mouth, as if,
Equal with stone, to me 'twould give

Its light and life.
        O restless thought,
Contented not! With 'Why' distraught.
Whom asked you then your riddle small? —
'If hither came no man at all

'Through this grey-green, sea-haunted lane,
Would it mere blackened naught remain?
Strives it this beauty and life to express
Only in human consciousness?

'Or, rather, idly breaks he in
To an Eden innocent of sin;
And, prouder than to be afraid,
Forgets his Maker in the made?'

Memory

When summer heat has drowsed the day
With blaze of noontide overhead,
And hidden greenfinch can but say
What but a moment since it said;
When harvest fields stand thick with wheat,
And wasp and bee slave — dawn till dark —
Nor home, till evening moonbeams beat,
Silvering the nightjar's oaken bark:
How strangely then the mind may build

36

A magic world of wintry cold,
Its meadows with frail frost-flowers filled —
Bright-ribbed with ice, a frozen wold! . . .

When dusk shuts in the shortest day,
And huge Orion spans the night;
Where antlered fireflames leap and play
Chequering the walls with fitful light —
Even sweeter in mind the summer's rose
May bloom again; her drifting swan
Resume her beauty; while rapture flows
Of birds long since to silence gone:
Beyond the Nowel, sharp and shrill,
Of Waits from out the snowbound street,
Drums to their fiddle beneath the hill
June's mill wheel where the waters meet . . .

O angel Memory that can
Double the joys of faithless Man!

The Fly

How large unto the tiny fly
    Must little things appear! —
A rosebud like a feather bed,
    Its prickle like a spear;

A dewdrop like a looking-glass,
    A hair like golden wire;
The smallest grain of mustard-seed
    As fierce as coals of fire;

A loaf of bread, a lofty hill;
    A wasp, a cruel leopard;
And specks of salt as bright to see
    As lambkins to a shepherd.

Jenny Wren

Of all the birds that rove and sing,
    Near dwellings made for men,
None is so nimble, feat, and trim
        As Jenny Wren.

With pin-point bill, and tail a-cock,
    So wildly shrill she cries,
The echoes on their roof-tree knock
        And fill the skies.

Never was sweeter seraph hid
    Within so small a house —
A tiny, inch-long, eager, ardent,
        Feathered mouse.

Trees

Of all the trees in England,
    Her sweet three corners in,
Only the Ash, the bonnie Ash
    Burns fierce while it is green.

Of all the trees in England,
    From sea to sea again,
The Willow loveliest stoops her boughs
    Beneath the driving rain.

Of all the trees in England,
    Past frankincense and myrrh,
There's none for smell, of bloom and smoke,
    Like Lime and Juniper.

Of all the trees in England,
    Oak, Elder, Elm and Thorn,
The Yew alone burns lamps of peace
    For them that lie forlorn.

Thunder

Call the cows home!
Call the cows home!
Louring storm clouds
Hitherward come;
East to West
Their wings are spread;
Lost in the blue
Is each heaven-high head;
They've dimmed the sun;
Turned day to night;
With a whistling wind
The woods are white;
Down streams the rain
On farm, barn, byre,
Bright green hill,
And bramble and brier,
Filling the valley
With glimmer and gloom:
Call the cows home!
Call the cows home!

The Storm

First there were two of us, then there were three of us,
Then there was one bird more,
Four of us — wild white sea-birds,
Treading the ocean floor;
And the *wind* rose, and the *sea* rose,
To the angry billows' roar —
With one of us — two of us — three of us — four of us
Sea-birds on the shore.

Soon there were five of us, soon there were nine of us,
And lo! in a trice sixteen!
And the yeasty surf curdled over the sands,
The gaunt grey rocks between;
And the tempest raved, and the lightning's fire
Struck blue on the spindrift hoar —
And on four of us — ay, and on four times four of us
Sea-birds on the shore.

And our sixteen waxed to thirty-two,
And they to past three score —
A wild, white welter of winnowing wings,
And ever more and more;
And the winds lulled, and the sea went down,
And the sun streamed out on high,
Gilding the pools and the spume and the spars
'Neath the vast blue deeps of the sky;

And the isles and the bright green headlands shone,
As they'd never shone before,
Mountains and valleys of silver cloud,
Wherein to swing, sweep, soar —
A host of screeching, scolding, scrabbling
Sea-birds on the shore —
A snowy, silent, sun-washed drift
Of sea-birds on the shore.

The Solitary Bird

Why should a bird in that solitary hollow
    Flying from east to west
Seem in the silence of the snow-blanched sunshine
    Gilding the valley's crest
Envoy and symbol of a past within me
    Centuries now at rest?

Shallowly arched the horizon looms beyond it,
    Turquoise green and blue;
Not even a whisper irks the magic of the evening
    The narrowing valley through;
No faintest echo brings a syllable revealing
    The secret once I knew:
Down *whsts* the snow again, cloud masks the
        sunshine —
    Bird gone, and memory too.

Titmouse

If you would happy company win,
Dangle a palm-nut from a tree,
Idly in green to sway and spin,
Its snow-pulped kernel for bait; and see
     A nimble titmouse enter in.

Out of earth's vast unknown of air,
Out of all summer, from wave to wave,
He'll perch, and prank his feathers fair,
Jangle a glass-clear wildering stave,
     And take his commons there —

This tiny son of life; this spright,
By momentary Human sought,
Plume will his wing in the dappling light,
Clash timbrel shrill and gay —
And into Time's enormous Nought,
     Sweet-fed will flit away.

A Goldfinch

This feather-soft creature
Tail to head,
Is golden yellow,
And black, and red.

A sip of water,
A twig to sing on,
A prong for nest,
The air to wing on,

A mate to love,
Some thistledown seed
Are all his joy, life,
Beauty, need.

Who?

1st Stranger: Who walks with us on the hills?
2nd Stranger: I cannot see for the mist.
3rd Stranger: Running water I hear,
            Keeping lugubrious tryst
            With its cresses and grasses and weeds,
            In the white obscure light from the sky.
2nd Stranger: *Who walks with us on the hills?*
Wild Bird: Ay! . . . Aye! . . . *Ay!* . . .

The Tower

There were no flowers among the stones of the
    wilderness.
I was standing alone by the green glazed tower,
Where among the cypresses winds went wandering,
Tinged now with gold-dust in the evening hour.

What goddess lingered here no tablet recorded;
Birds wild with beauty sang from ilex and yew;
Afar rose the chasms and glaciers of mountains,
The snow of their summits wax-wan in the blue —

In the blue of the heights of the heavenly vacancy —
My companions the silence, the relics, the lost;
And that speechless, divine, invisible influence,
Remote as the stars in the vague of the Past.

43

The Mountains

Still and blanched and cold and lone
   The icy hills far off from me
With frosty ulys overgrown
   Stand in their sculptured secrecy.

No path of theirs the chamois fleet
   Treads, with a nostril to the wind;
O'er their ice-marbled glaciers beat
   No wings of eagles in my mind —

Yea, in my mind these mountains rise,
   Their perils dyed with evening's rose;
And still my ghost sits at my eyes
   And thirsts for their untroubled snows.

The Vacant Farmhouse

Three gables; clustered chimney-stacks; a wall
Snowed every Spring with cherry, gage, and pear,
Now suckered, rank, unpruned. Green-seeded, tall,
A drift of sullen nettles souring near —
Beside a staved-in stye and green-scummed pond,
Where once duck-dabbled sunshine rippled round.

Dark empty barns; a shed; abandoned byres;
A weedy stack-yard whence all life has fled;
A derelict wain, with loose and rusted tyres;
And an enormous elm-tree overhead . . .

That attic casement. . . . Was there flaw in the glass? . . .
I thought, as I glanced up, there had peered a face.
But no. Still: eyes are strange; for at my steady stare
Through the cool sunlit evening air,
Scared silent sparrows flew up out of the ivy there
Into an elder tree — for perching-place.

The Old Summerhouse

This blue-washed, old, thatched summerhouse —
Paint scaling, and fading from its walls —
How often from its hingeless door
I have watched — dead leaf, like the ghost of a mouse,
Rasping the worn brick floor —
The snows of the weir descending below,
And their thunderous waterfall.

Fall — fall: dark, garrulous rumour,
Until I could listen no more.
Could listen no more — for beauty with sorrow
Is a burden hard to be borne:
The evening light on the foam, and the swans, there;
That music, remote, forlorn.

Nicholas Nye

Thistle and darnel and dock grew there,
    And a bush, in the corner, of may,
On the orchard wall I used to sprawl
    In the blazing heat of the day;
Half asleep and half awake,
    While the birds went twittering by,
And nobody there my lone to share
    But Nicholas Nye.

Nicholas Nye was lean and grey,
    Lame of a leg and old,
More than a score of donkey's years
    He had seen since he was foaled;
He munched the thistles, purple and spiked,
    Would sometimes stoop and sigh,
And turn his head, as if he said,
    'Poor Nicholas Nye!'

45

Alone with his shadow he'd drowse in the meadow,
    Lazily swinging his tail,
At the break of day he used to bray, —
    Not much too hearty and hale;
But a wonderful gumption was under his skin,
    And a clear calm light in his eye,
And once in a while: he'd smile . . .
        Would Nicholas Nye.

Seem to be smiling at me, he would,
    From his bush in the corner, of may, —
Bony and ownerless, widowed and worn,
    Knobble-kneed, lonely and grey;
And over the grass would seem to pass
    'Neath the deep dark blue of the sky,
Something much better than words between me
        And Nicholas Nye.

But dusk would come in the apple boughs,
    The green of the glow-worm shine,
The birds in nest would crouch to rest,
    And home I'd trudge to mine;
And there, in the moonlight, dark with dew,
    Asking not wherefore nor why,
Would brood like a ghost, and as still as a post,
        Old Nicholas Nye.

The Railway Junction

From here through tunnelled gloom the track
Forks into two; and one of these
Wheels onward into darkening hills,
And one toward distant seas.

How still it is; the signal light
At set of sun shines palely green;
A thrush sings; other sound there's none,
Nor traveller to be seen —

Where late there was a throng. And now,
In peace awhile, I sit alone;
Though soon, at the appointed hour,
I shall myself be gone.

But not their way: the bow-legged groom,
The parson in black, the widow and son,
The sailor with his cage, the gaunt
Gamekeeper with his gun,

That fair one, too, discreetly veiled —
All, who so mutely came, and went,
Will reach those far nocturnal hills,
Or shores, ere night is spent.

I nothing know why thus we met —
Their thoughts, their longings, hopes, their fate:
And what shall I remember, except —
The evening growing late —

That here through tunnelled gloom the track
Forks into two; of these
One into darkening hills leads on,
And one toward distant seas?

47

The Corner Stone

Sterile these stones
By time in ruin laid.
Yet many a creeping thing
Its haven has made
In these least crannies, where falls
Dark's dew, and noonday shade.

The claw of the tender bird
Finds lodgement here;
Dye-winged butterflies poise;
Emmet and beetle steer
Their busy course; the bee
Drones, laden, near.

Their myriad-mirrored eyes
Great day reflect.
By their exquisite farings
Is this granite specked;
Is trodden to infinite dust;
By gnawing lichens decked.

Toward what eventual dream
Sleeps its cold on,
When into ultimate dark
These lives shall be gone,
And even of man not a shadow remain
Of all he has done?

Lone

Shrill rang the squeak in the empty house
Of the sharp-nosed mouse, the hungry mouse.

'Sing, sing: here none doth dwell!'
Dripped the water in the well.

A robin on the shepherd's grave
Whistled a solitary stave.

And, 'Lone-lone!' the curlew cried,
Scolding the sheep-strewn mountain's side.

Nothing

Whsst, and away, and over the green,
Scampered a shape that never was seen.
It ran without sound, it ran without shadow,
Never a grass-blade in unmown meadow
Stooped at the thistledown fall of its foot.
I watched it vanish, yet saw it not —
A moment past, it had gazed at me;
Now nought but myself and the spindle tree.
A nothing! — Of air? Of earth? Of sun? —
From emptiness come, into vacancy gone! . . . .
Whsst, and away, and over the green,
Scampered a shape that never was seen.

Summer Evening

The sandy cat by the Farmer's chair
Mews at his knee for dainty fare;
Old Rover in his moss-greened house
Mumbles a bone, and barks at a mouse.
In the dewy fields the cattle lie
Chewing the cud 'neath a fading sky;
Dobbin at manger pulls his hay:
Gone is another summer's day.

Martins: September

At secret daybreak they had met —
    Chill mist beneath the welling light
Screening the marshes green and wet —
    An ardent legion wild for flight.

Each preened and sleeked an arrowlike wing;
    Their eager throats with lapsing cries
Praising whatever fate might bring —
    Cold wave, or Africa's paradise.

Unventured, trackless leagues of air;
    England's sweet summer narrowing on;
Her lovely pastures: nought their care —
    Only this ardour to be gone.

A tiny, elfin, ecstatic host . . .
    And 'neath them, on the highway's crust,
Like some small mute belated ghost,
    A sparrow pecking in the dust.

Winter

Green Mistletoe!
Oh, I remember now
A dell of snow,
Frost on the bough;
None there but I:
Snow, snow, and a wintry sky.

None there but I,
And footprints one by one,
Zigzaggedly,
Where I had run;
Where shrill and powdery
A robin sat in the tree.

And he whistled sweet;
And I in the crusted snow
With snow-clubbed feet
Jigged to and fro,
Till, from the day,
The rose-light ebbed away.

And the robin flew
Into the air, the air,
The white mist through;
And small and rare
The night-frost fell
Into the calm and misty dell.

And the dusk gathered low,
And the silver moon and stars
On the frozen snow
Drew taper bars,
Kindled winking fires
In the hooded briers.

And the sprawling Bear
Growled deep in the sky;
And Orion's hair
Streamed sparkling by:
But the North sighed low:
'*Snow, snow, more snow!*'

The Snowflake

See, now, this filigree: 'tis snow,
Shaped, in the void, of heavenly dew;
On winds of space like flower to blow
In a wilderness of blue.

Black are those pines. The utter cold
Hath frozen to silence the birds' green woods.
Rime hath ensteeled the wormless mould,
A vacant quiet broods.

Lo, this entrancèd thing! — a breath
Of life that bids Man's heart to crave
Still for perfection: ere fall death,
And earth shut in his grave.

Ice

The North Wind sighed:
And in a trice
What was water
Now is ice.

What sweet rippling
Water was
Now bewitched is
Into glass:

White and brittle
Where is seen
The prisoned milfoil's
Tender green;

Clear and ringing,
With sun aglow,
Where the boys sliding
And skating go.

Now furred's each stick
And stalk and blade
With crystals out of
Dewdrops made.

Worms and ants
Flies, snails and bees
Keep close house-guard,
Lest they freeze;

Oh, with how sad
And solemn an eye
Each fish stares up
Into the sky.

In dread lest his
Wide watery home
At night shall solid
Ice become.

A Robin

Ghost-grey the fall of night,
    Ice-bound the lane,
Lone in the dying light
    Flits he again;
Lurking where shadows steal,
Perched in his coat of blood,
Man's homestead at his heel,
    Death-still the wood.

Odd restless child; it's dark;
    All wings are flown
But this one wizard's — hark!
    Stone clapped on stone!
Changeling and solitary,
Secret and sharp and small,
Flits he from tree to tree,
    Calling on all.

The Fire

Loud roared the flames
On Bonner's heath,
But all was crudded
Snow beneath,
Save where in shadow,
Clip — clop — clupp,
He stumbled down
Who had stolen up.

Comfort

As I mused by the hearthside,
    Puss said to me:
'There burns the Fire, man,
    And here sit we.

'Four Walls around us
    Against the cold air;
And the latchet drawn close
    To the draughty Stair.

'A Roof o'er our heads
    Star-proof, moon immune,
And a wind in the chimney
    To wail us a tune.

'What Felicity!' miaowed he,
    'Where none may intrude;
Just Man and Beast — met
    In this Solitude!

'Dear God, what security,
    Comfort and bliss!
And to think, too, what ages
    Have brought us to this!

'You in your sheep's-wool coat,
    Buttons of bone,
And me in my fur-about
    On the warm hearthstone.'

The Moth

Isled in the midnight air,
Musked with the dark's faint bloom,
Out into glooming and secret haunts
    The flame cries, 'Come!'

Lovely in dye and fan,
A-tremble in shimmering grace,
A moth from her winter swoon
    Uplifts her face:

Stares from her glamorous eyes;
Wafts her on plumes like mist;
In ecstasy swirls and sways
    To her strange tryst.

Nobody Knows

Often I've heard the Wind sigh
  By the ivied orchard wall,
Over the leaves in the dark night,
  Breathe a sighing call,
And faint away in the silence,
  While I, in my bed,
Wondered, 'twixt dreaming and waking,
    What it said.

Nobody knows what the Wind is,
  Under the height of the sky,
Where the hosts of the stars keep far away house
  And its wave sweeps by —
Just a great wave of the air,
  Tossing the leaves in its sea,
And foaming under the eaves of the roof
    That covers me.

And so we live under deep water,
  All of us, beasts and men,
And our bodies are buried down under the sand,
  When we go again;
And leave, like the fishes, our shells,
  And float on the wind and away,
To where, o'er the marvellous tides of the air,
    Burns day.

Unforeseen

Darkness had fallen. I opened the door:
And lo, a stranger in the empty room —
A marvel of moonlight upon wall and floor . . .
The quiet of mercy? Or the hush of doom?

Stars

If to the heavens you lift your eyes
When Winter reigns o'er our Northern skies,
And snow-cloud none the zenith mars,
At Yule-tide midnight these your stars:
Low in the South see bleak-blazing Sirius;
Above him hang Betelgeuse, Procyon wan;
Wild-eyed to West of him, Rigel and Bellatrix,
And rudd-red Aldebaran journeying on.
High in night's roof-tree beams twinkling Capella;
Vega and Deneb prowl low in the North;
Far to the East roves the Lion-heart, Regulus;
While the twin sons of Zeus to'rd the zenith gleam forth.

But when Midsummer Eve in man's sleep-drowsed hours
Refreshes for daybreak its dew-bright flowers,
Though three of these Night Lights aloft remain,
For nine, if you gaze, you will gaze in vain.
Yet comfort find, for, far-shining there,
See golden Arcturus and cold Altaïr;
Crystalline Spica, and, strange to scan,
Blood-red Antares, foe to Man.

II

The Children of Stare

Winter is fallen early
On the house of Stare ;
Birds in reverberating flocks
   Haunt its ancestral box ;
   Bright are the plenteous berries
   In clusters in the air.

Still is the fountain's music,
   The dark pool icy still,
Whereupon a small and sanguine sun
   Floats in a mirror on,
   Into a West of crimson,
   From a South of daffodil.

'Tis strange to see young children
   In such a wintry house ;
Like rabbits' on the frozen snow
   Their tell-tale footprints go ;
   Their laughter rings like timbrels
   'Neath evening ominous :

Their small and heightened faces
   Like wine-red winter buds ;
Their frolic bodies gentle as
   Flakes in the air that pass,
   Frail as the twirling petal
   From the briar of the woods.

Above them silence lours,
  Still as an arctic sea;
Light fails; night falls; the wintry moon
  Glitters; the crocus soon
  Will open grey and distracted
  On earth's austerity:

Thick mystery, wild peril,
  Law like an iron rod: —
Yet sport they on in Spring's attire,
  Each with his tiny fire
  Blown to a core of ardour
  By the awful breath of God.

The Dunce

Why does he still keep ticking?
  Why does his round white face
Stare at me over the books and ink,
  And mock at my disgrace?
Why does that thrush call, 'Dunce, dunce, dunce!'?
  Why does that bluebottle buzz?
Why does the sun so silent shine? —
  And what do I care if it does?

Idleness

I saw old Idleness, fat, with great cheeks
Puffed to the huge circumference of a sigh,
But past all tinge of apples long ago.
His boyish fingers twiddled up and down
The filthy remnant of a cup of physic
That thicked in odour all the while he stayed.

His eyes were sad as fishes that swim up
And stare upon an element not theirs
Through a thin skin of shrewish water, then
Turn on a languid fin, and dip down, down,
Into unplumbed, vast, oozy deeps of dream.
His stomach was his master, and proclaimed it;
And never were such meagre puppets made
The slaves of such a tyrant, as his thoughts
Of that obese epitome of ills.

Trussed up he sat, the mockery of himself;
And when upon the wan green of his eye
I marked the gathering lustre of a tear,
Thought I myself must weep, until I caught
A grey, smug smile of satisfaction smirch
His pallid features at his misery.
And laugh did I, to see the little snares
He had set for pests to vex him: his great feet
Prisoned in greater boots; so narrow a stool
To seat such elephantine parts as his;
Ay, and the book he read, a Hebrew Bible;
And, to incite a gross and backward wit,
An old, crabbed, wormed, Greek dictionary; and
A foxy Ovid bound in dappled calf.

John Mouldy

I spied John Mouldy in his cellar,
Deep down twenty steps of stone;
In the dusk he sat a-smiling,
    Smiling there alone.

He read no book, he snuffed no candle;
The rats ran in, the rats ran out;
And far and near, the drip of water
    Went whisp'ring about.

The dusk was still, with dew a-falling,
I saw the Dog-star bleak and grim,
I saw a slim brown rat of Norway
    Creep over him.

I spied John Mouldy in his cellar,
Deep down twenty steps of stone;
In the dusk he sat a-smiling,
    Smiling there alone.

Pooh!

Dainty Miss Apathy
Sat on a sofa,
Dangling her legs,
And with nothing to do;
She looked at a drawing of
Old Queen Victoria,
At a rug from far Persia —
An exquisite blue;
At a bowl of bright tulips;
A needlework picture
Of doves caged in wicker
You could almost hear coo;
She looked at the switch
That evokes e-
Lectricity;
At the coals of an age
B.C. millions and two —
When the trees were like ferns
And the reptiles all flew;
She looked at the cat
Asleep on the hearthrug,
At the sky at the window, —
The clouds in it, too;

And a marvellous light
From the West burning through:
And the one silly word
In her desolate noddle
As she dangled her legs,
Having nothing to do,
Was not, as you'd guess,
Of dumfoundered felicity,
But contained just four letters,
And these pronounced *POOH!*

Miss T.

It's a very odd thing —
  As odd as can be —
That whatever Miss T. eats
  Turns into Miss T.;
Porridge and apples,
  Mince, muffins and mutton,
Jam, junket, jumbles —
  Not a rap, not a button
It matters; the moment
  They're out of her plate,
Though shared by Miss Butcher
  And sour Mr. Bate,
Tiny and cheerful,
  And neat as can be,
Whatever Miss T. eats
  Turns into Miss T.

The Old Angler

Twilight leaned mirrored in a pool
  Where willow boughs swept green and hoar,
Silk-clear the water, calm and cool,
  Silent the weedy shore:

There in abstracted, brooding mood
  One fishing sate. His painted float
Motionless as a planet stood;
  Motionless his boat.

A melancholy soul was this,
  With lantern jaw, gnarled hand, vague eye;
Huddled in pensive solitariness
  He had fished existence by.

Empty his creel; stolen his bait —
  Impassively he angled on,
Though mist now showed the evening late
  And daylight wellnigh gone.

Suddenly, like a tongueless bell,
  Downward his gaudy cork did glide;
A deep, low-gathering, gentle swell
  Spread slowly far and wide.

Wheeped out his tackle from noiseless winch,
  And furtive as a thief, his thumb,
With nerve intense, wound inch by inch
  A line no longer numb.

What fabulous spoil could thus unplayed
  Gape upward to a mortal air? —
He stoops engrossed; his tanned cheek greyed;
  His heart stood still: for there,

Wondrously fairing, beneath the skin
  Of secretly bubbling water seen,
Swims, not the silver of scale and fin —
  But gold inmixt with green.

Deeply astir in oozy bed,
  The darkening mirror ripples and rocks:
And lo — a wan-pale, lovely head,
  Hook tangled in its locks!

Cold from her haunt — a Naiad slim.
  Shoulder and cheek gleamed ivory white;
Though now faint stars stood over him,
  The hour hard on night.

Her green eyes gazed like one half-blind
  In sudden radiance; her breast
Breathed the sweet air, while gently twined,
  'Gainst the cold water pressed,

Her lean webbed hands. She floated there,
  Light as a scentless petalled flower,
Water-drops dewing from her hair
  In tinkling beadlike shower.

So circling sidelong, her tender throat
  Uttered a grieving, desolate wail;
Shrill o'er the dark pool lapsed its note,
  Piteous as nightingale.

Ceased Echo. And he? — a life's remorse
  Welled to a tongue unapt to charm,
But never a word broke harsh and hoarse
  To quiet her alarm.

With infinite stealth his twitching thumb
  Tugged softly at the tautened gut,
Bubble-light, fair, her lips now dumb,
  She moved, and struggled not;

But with set, wild, unearthly eyes
   Pale-gleaming, fixed as if in fear,
She couched in the water, with quickening sighs
   And floated near.

In hollow heaven the stars were at play;
   Wan glow-worms greened the pool-side grass;
Dipped the wide-bellied boat. His prey
   Gazed on; nor breathed. Alas! —

Long sterile years had come and gone;
   Youth, like a distant dream, was sped;
Heart, hope, and eyes had hungered on. . . .
   He turned a shaking head,

And clumsily groped amid the gold,
   Sleek with night dews, of that tangling hair,
Till pricked his finger keen and cold
   The barb embedded there.

Teeth clenched, he drew his knife — 'Snip, snip,' —
   Groaned, and sate shivering back; and she,
Treading the water with birdlike dip,
   Shook her sweet shoulders free:

Drew backward, smiling, infatuate fair,
   His life's disasters in her eyes,
All longing and folly, grief, despair,
   Daydreams and mysteries.

She stooped her brow; laid low her cheek,
   And, steering on that silk-tressed craft,
Out from the listening, leaf-hung creek,
   Tossed up her chin, and laughed —

A mocking, icy, inhuman note.
  One instant flashed that crystal breast,
Leaned, and was gone. Dead-still the boat:
  And the deep dark at rest.

Flits moth to flower. A water-rat
  Noses the placid ripple. And lo!
Streams a lost meteor. Night is late,
  And daybreak zephyrs flow. . . .

And he — the cheated? Dusk till morn,
  Insensate, even of hope forsook,
He muttering squats, aloof, forlorn,
  Dangling a baitless hook.

The Scarecrow

All winter through I bow my head
  Beneath the driving rain;
The North Wind powders me with snow
  And blows me black again;
At midnight in a maze of stars
  I flame with glittering rime,
And stand, above the stubble, stiff
  As mail at morning-prime.
But when that child, called Spring, and all
  His host of children, come,
Scattering their buds and dew upon
  These acres of my home,
Some rapture in my rags awakes;
  I lift void eyes and scan
The skies for crows, those ravening foes,
  Of my strange master, Man.

I watch him striding lank behind
   His clashing team, and know
Soon will the wheat swish body high
   Where once lay sterile snow;
Soon shall I gaze across a sea
   Of sun-begotten grain,
Which my unflinching watch hath sealed
   For harvest once again.

The Huntsmen

Three jolly gentlemen,
   In coats of red,
Rode their horses
   Up to bed.

Three jolly gentlemen
   Snored till morn,
Their horses champing
   The golden corn.

Three jolly gentlemen,
   At break of day,
Came clitter-clatter down the stairs
   And galloped away.

'Please to Remember'

Here am I,
A poor old Guy:
Legs in a bonfire,
Head in the sky,

Shoeless my toes,
Wild stars behind,
Smoke in my nose,
And my eye-peeps blind;

Old hat, old straw —
In this disgrace;
While the wildfire gleams
On a mask for face.

Ay, all I am made of
Only trash is;
And soon — soon,
Will be dust and ashes.

The Snow-man

What shape is this in cowl of snow?
  Stiff broom and icy hat?
A saffron moon, half-hidden, stares —
  But what is she staring *at?*

The knocker dangles on the door,
  But stark as tree and post
He blankly eyes the bright green paint,
  Is silent as a ghost.

But wait till belfry midnight strike,
    And up to the stars is tossed
Shrill cockcrow ! — *then,* he'll gadding go —
    And, at his heels, Jack Frost :

Broom over shoulder, away he'll go,
    Finger-tips tingling, nose aglow,
Dancing and yodelling through the snow,
    And, at his heels, Jack Frost !

Lob-Lie-by-the-Fire

Keep me a crust
Or starve I must ;
Hoard me a bone
Or I am gone ;
A handful of coals
Leave red for me ;
Or the smouldering log
Of a wild-wood tree ;
Even a kettle
To sing on the hob
Will comfort the heart
Of poor old Lob :
Then with his hairy
Hands he'll bless
Prosperous master,
And kind mistress.

Never More, Sailor

Never more, Sailor,
Shalt thou be
Tossed on the wind-ridden,
Restless sea.
Its tides may labour;
All the world
Shake 'neath that weight
Of waters hurled:
But its whole shock
Can only stir
Thy dust to a quiet
Even quieter.
Thou mock'st at land
Who now art come
To such a small
And shallow home;
Yet bore the sea
Full many a care
For bones that once
A sailor's were.
And though the grave's
Deep soundlessness
Thy once sea-deafened
Ear distress,
No robin ever
On the deep
Hopped with his song
To haunt thy sleep.

A Still Life

Bottle, coarse tumbler, loaf of bread,
Cheap paper, a lean long kitchen knife:
No moral, no problem, sermon, or text,
No hint of a Why, Whence, Whither, of If;
Mere workaday objects put into paint —
Bottle and tumbler, loaf and knife. . . .
And engrossed, round-spectacled Chardin's
        Passion for life.

Thomas Hardy

Mingled the moonlight with daylight — the last in the narrowing
        west;
Silence of nightfall lay over the shallowing valleys at rest
        In the Earth's green breast:
Yet a small multitudinous singing, a lully of voices of birds,
Unseen in the vague shelving hollows, welled up with my
        questioning words:
All Dorsetshire's larks for connivance of sweetness seemed trysting
        to greet
Him in whose song the bodings of raven and nightingale meet.

Stooping and smiling, he questioned, 'No birdnotes myself do I
        hear?
Perhaps 'twas the talk of chance farers, abroad in the hush with us
        here —
        In the dusk-light clear?'
And there peered from his eyes, as I listened, a concourse of
        women and men,
Whom his words had made living, long-suffering — they flocked
        to remembrance again;
'O Master,' I cried in my heart, 'lorn thy tidings, grievous thy
        song;
Yet thine, too, this solacing music, as we earthfolk stumble along.'

III

Reflections

So much herself she is that when she is near
All love-delighting things are thrice as dear;
And even the thought of her when she is far
Narcissus is, and they the water are.

Swallows Flown

Whence comes that small continuous silence
    Haunting the livelong day?
This void, where a sweetness, so seldom heeded,
    Once ravished my heart away?
As if a loved one, too little valued,
    Had vanished — could not stay?

Quiet

Mutely the mole toils on;
The worm in silk cocoon
Stealthy as spider spins,
        As glides the moon.
But listen where envy peers 'neath the half-closed lid;
Where peeping vanity lurks; where pride lies hid;
And peace beyond telling share with the light-stilled eye,
When nought but an image of the loved one's nigh.

She Said

She said, 'I will come back again
     As soon as breaks the morn.'
But the lark was wearying of the blue,
     The dew dry on the thorn;
     And all was still forlorn.

She said, 'I will come back again,
     At the first quick stroke of noon.'
But the birds were hid in the shade from the heat
     When the clock tolled, *No : but soon!*
     And then beat slowly on.

She said, 'Yes, I'll be back again
     Before the sun has set.'
But the sweetest promises often made
     Are the easiest to forget,
     No matter grief and fret. . . .

That moon, now silvering the east,
     One shadow casts — my own.
Thought I, My friend, how often we
Have shared this solitude. And see,
     Midnight will soon draw on,
When the last leaf of hope is fallen,
And silence haunts heart's vacancy,
       And even pining's done.

The Tryst

'O whither are you faring to, my sweetheart?
How far now are you journeying, my dear?'
'I am climbing to the brink of yonder hill-top,
Naught human far or near.'

'And what will you be seeking there, my sweetheart?
What happy scene is thence surveyed, my dear?'
' 'Twill be night-tide when outwearied I come thither,
And star-shine icy-clear.'

'But what will you be brooding on, my sweetheart?
What fantasies of darkness will appear?'
'My self will keep a tryst there — bleak and lonely —
My own heart's secrets I shall share.'

'But what will be the manner of your greeting?
What word will you then whisper — no one near?'
'Ah, he who loved me once would know the answer,
Were he still true, my dear.'

Autumn

There is a wind where the rose was;
Cold rain where sweet grass was;
   And clouds like sheep
   Stream o'er the steep
Grey skies where the lark was.

Nought gold where your hair was;
Nought warm where your hand was;
   But phantom, forlorn,
   Beneath the thorn,
Your ghost where your face was.

Sad winds where your voice was;
Tears, tears where my heart was;
   And ever with me,
   Child, ever with me,
Silence where hope was.

Adieu

Had these eyes never seen you,
This heart kept its paces,
If this mind — flooded river —
Had glassed not your graces;
Though lone my cold pillow,
In peace I had slumbered,
Whose hours now of waking
By moments are numbered.

You came; ice-still, asp-like;
You glanced 'neath your lashes;
You smiled — and you sighed out
Life's flame into ashes.
No compassion you showed me,
Void breast, cheating laughter:
Now I swing to my tryst
From this night-clotted rafter.

Peep out with your eyes.
Pout your mouth. Tilt your nose.
'Gainst the stench and the flies
Cull a balm-sprig, a rose.
This tongue that is stilled —
Not a tremor! Oh, else,
The whole roof of heaven
   Would cry, False!

The Changeling

'Ahoy, and ahoy!'
  'Twixt mocking and merry —
'Ahoy and ahoy, there,
  Young man of the ferry!'
She stood on the steps
  In the watery gloom —
That Changeling — 'Ahoy, there!'
  She called him to come.
He came on the green wave,
  He came on the grey,
Where stooped that sweet lady
  That still summer's day.

He fell in a dream
    Of her beautiful face,
As she sat on the thwart
    And smiled in her place.
No echo his oar woke,
    Float silent did they,
Past low-grazing cattle
    In the sweet of the hay.
And still in a dream
    At her beauty sat he,
Drifting stern foremost
    Down — down to the sea.
Come you, then: call,
    When the twilight apace
Brings shadow to brood
    On the loveliest face;
You shall hear o'er the water
    Ring faint in the grey —
'Ahoy, and ahoy, there!'
    And tremble away;
'Ahoy, and ahoy!...'
    And tremble away.

Divided

Two spheres on meeting may so softly collide
They stay, as if still kissing, side by side.
Lovers may part for ever — the cause so small
Not even a lynx could see a gap at all.

An Epitaph

Last, Stone, a little yet;
And then this dust forget.
But thou, fair Rose, bloom on.
For she who is gone
Was lovely too; nor would she grieve to be
Sharing in solitude her dreams with thee.

Belated

Once gay, now sad; remote — and dear;
Why turn away in doubt and fear?
I search again your grieved self-pitying face;
Kindness sits clouded there. But, love? No, not a trace.

What wonder this? Mine not to scold.
You, in so much a child; and I, how old!
Who know how rare on earth your like must be:
There's nought commensurate, alas, in age or me.

Bare ruined choirs — though time may grace
      bestow
On such poor relics in eve's after-glow;
And even to age serenity may bring,
Where birds may haven find; and peace; though not
      to sing.

But ah, blest Light-of-Morning One,
Ev'n though my life were nearly done?
Ev'n though no mortal power could that delay?
Think of the lightless journey thither — you away!

IV

Maerchen

Soundless the moth-flit, crisp the death-watch tick;
Crazed in her shaken arbour bird did sing;
Slow wreathed the grease adown from soot-clogged wick:
  The Cat looked long and softly at the King.

Mouse frisked and scampered, leapt, gnawed, squeaked;
Small at the window looped cowled bat a-wing;
The dim-lit rafters with the night-mist reeked:
  The Cat looked long and softly at the King.

O wondrous robe enstarred, in night dyed deep:
O air scarce-stirred with the Court's far junketing:
O stagnant Royalty — A-swoon? Asleep?
  The Cat looked long and softly at the King.

The Mocking Fairy

'Won't you look out of your window, Mrs. Gill?'
  Quoth the Fairy, nidding, nodding in the garden;
'Can't you look out of your window, Mrs. Gill?'
  Quoth the Fairy, laughing softly in the garden;
But the air was still, the cherry boughs were still,
And the ivy-tod neath the empty sill,
And never from her window looked out Mrs. Gill
  On the Fairy shrilly mocking in the garden.

'What have they done with you, you poor Mrs. Gill?'
　　Quoth the Fairy brightly glancing in the garden;
'Where have they hidden you, you poor old Mrs. Gill?'
　　Quoth the Fairy dancing lightly in the garden;
But night's faint veil now wrapped the hill,
Stark 'neath the stars stood the dead-still Mill,
And out of her cold cottage never answered Mrs. Gill
　　The Fairy mimbling, mambling in the garden.

The Ogre

'Tis moonlight on Trebarwith Sands,
　　And moonlight on their seas,
Lone in a cove a cottage stands
　　Enclustered in with trees.

Snuffing its thin faint smoke afar
　　An Ogre prowls, and he
Smells supper; for where humans are,
　　Rich dainties too may be.

Sweet as a larder to a mouse,
　　So to him staring down,
Seemed the small-windowed moonlit house,
　　With jasmine overgrown.

He snorted, as the billows snort
　　In darkness of the night,
Betwixt his lean locks tawny-swart,
　　He glowered on the sight.

Into the garden sweet with peas
　　He put his wooden shoe,
And bending back the apple trees
　　Crept covetously through;

82

Then, stooping, with an impious eye
　　Stared through the lattice small,
And spied two children which did lie
　　Asleep, against the wall.

Into their dreams no shadow fell
　　Of his disastrous thumb
Groping discreet, and gradual,
　　Across the quiet room.

But scarce his nail had scraped the cot
　　Wherein these children lay,
As if his malice were forgot,
　　It suddenly did stay.

For faintly in the ingle-nook
　　He heard a cradle-song,
That rose into his thoughts and woke
　　Terror them among.

For she who in the kitchen sat
　　Darning by the fire,
Guileless of what he would be at,
　　Sang sweet as wind or wire : —

'Lullay, thou little tiny child,
　　By-by, lullay, lullie ;
Jesu in glory, meek and mild,
　　This night remember thee !

'Fiend, witch, and goblin, foul and wild,
　　He deems them smoke to be ;
Lullay, thou little tiny child,
　　By-by, lullay, lullie !'

The Ogre lifted up his eyes
　　Into the moon's pale ray,
And gazed upon her leopard-wise,
　　Cruel and clear as day ;

He snarled in gluttony and fear —
   The wind blows dismally —
'Jesu in storm my lambs be near,
   By-by, lullay, lullie !'

And like a ravenous beast which sees
   The hunter's icy eye,
So did this wretch in wrath confess
   Sweet Jesu's mastery.

With gaunt locks dangling, crouched he, then
   Drew backward from his prey,
Through tangled apple-boughs again
   He wrenched and rent his way.

Out on Trebarwith Sands he broke,
   The waves yelled back his cry,
Gannet and cormorant echo woke
   As he went striding by.

The Supper

A Wolf he pricks with eyes of fire
Across the dark, frost-crusted snows,
   Seeking his prey,
   He pads his way
Where Jane benighted goes,
   Where Jane benighted goes.

He curdles the bleak air with ire,
Ruffling his hoary raiment through,
   And lo ! he sees
   Beneath the trees
Where Jane's light footprints go,
   Where Jane's light footprints go.

No hound peals thus in wicked joy,
He snaps his muzzle in the snows,
    His five-clawed feet
    Now scamper fleet
Where Jane's bright lanthorn shows,
  Where Jane's bright lanthorn shows.

His hungry face stares out unseen
On hers as pure as wilding rose,
    Her amber eyes
    In fear's surprise
Watch largely as she goes,
  Watch largely as she goes.

Salt wells his hunger in his jaws,
His lust it revels to and fro
    Yet small beneath
    A soft voice saith,
'Jane shall in safety go,
  Jane shall in safety go.'

He lurched as if a fiery lash
Had scourged his hide, and through, and through
    His furious eyes
    O'erscanned the skies,
But nearer dared not go,
  But nearer dared not go.

He reared like wild Bucephalus,
His fangs like spears in him uprose,
    Ev'n to the town
    Jane's flitting gown
He grins on as she goes,
  He grins on as she goes.

In fierce lament he howls amain,
He scampers, marvelling in his throes
    What brought him there
    To sup on air,
While Jane unharmèd goes,
  While Jane unharmèd goes.

The Mermaids

Sand, sand; hills of sand;
  And the wind where nothing is
Green and sweet of the land;
  No grass, no trees,
  No bird, no butterfly,
But hills, hills of sand,
  And a burning sky.

Sea, sea; mounds of the sea,
  Hollow, and dark, and blue,
Flashing incessantly
  The whole sea through;
  No flower, no jutting root,
Only the floor of the sea,
  With foam afloat.

Blow, blow, winding shells;
  And the watery fish,
Deaf to the hidden bells,
  In the waters plash;
No streaming gold, no eyes,
  Watching along the waves,
But far-blown shells, faint bells,
  From the darkling caves.

I Saw Three Witches

I saw three witches
That bowed down like barley,
And took to their brooms 'neath a louring sky,
And, mounting a storm-cloud,
Aloft on its margin,
Stood black in the silver as up they did fly.

I saw three witches
That mocked the poor sparrows
They carried in cages of wicker along,
Till a hawk from his eyrie
Swooped down like an arrow,
And smote on the cages, and ended their song.

I saw three witches
That sailed in a shallop
All turning their heads with a truculent smile
Till a bank of green osiers
Concealed their grim faces,
Though I heard them lamenting for many a mile.

I saw three witches
Asleep in a valley,
Their heads in a row, like stones in a flood,
Till the moon, creeping upward,
Looked white through the valley,
And turned them to bushes in bright scarlet bud.

The Old King

Woke — the old King of Cumberland:
  Yet breathed not nor stirred,
But crouched in the darkness, hearkening after
  A voice he had heard.

He leaned upon his foursquare bed,
  Thumb beneath bristling chin;
'Alas, alas! — the woeful dream —
  The dream that I was in!'

The old, old King of Cumberland
  Muttered, ' 'Twas not the sea
Gushing upon Schlievlisskin rocks
  That wakened me.

'Thunder from midmost night it was not,
  For yonder at those bars
Burn fiercely toward the Eastern deeps
  The summer stars.'

The old, old King of Cumberland
  Mused yet, 'Rats ever did
Ramp, rustle, clink my spurs, and gnaw
  My coverlid.

'Oft hath a furtive midnight breeze
  Along this valance skirred;
But in this stagnant calm 'twas not
  The wind I heard.

'Some keener, stranger, quieter, closer
    Voice it was me woke . . .'
And silence, like a billow, drowned
    The word he spoke.

Fixed now his stare, for limned in dark,
    Gazing from cowl-like hood,
Stark in the vague, all-listening night,
    A shadow stood.

Sudden a gigantic hand he thrust
    Into his bosom cold,
Where now no surging restless beat
    Its long tale told.

Swept on him then, as there he sate,
    Terror icy chill:
'Twas silence that had him awoke —
    His heart stood still.

Never-To-Be

Down by the waters of the sea
Reigns the King of Never-to-be.
His palace walls are black with night;
His torches star and moon's light,
And for his timepiece deep and grave
Beats on the green unhastening wave.

Windswept are his high corridors;
His pleasance the sea-mantled shores;
For sentinel a shadow stands
With hair in heaven, and cloudy hands;
And round his bed, king's guards to be,
Watch pines in iron solemnity.

His hound is mute; his steed at will
Roams pastures deep with asphodel;
His queen is to her slumber gone;
His courtiers mute lie, hewn in stone;
He hath forgot where he did hide
His sceptre in the mountain-side.

Grey-capped and muttering, mad is he —
The childless King of Never-to-be;
For all his people in the deep
Keep, everlasting, fast asleep;
And all his realm is foam and rain,
Whispering of what comes not again.

The Thief at Robin's Castle

There came a Thief one night to Robin's Castle,
    He climbed up into a Tree;
And sitting with his head among the branches,
    A wondrous Sight did see.

For there was Robin supping at his table,
    With Candles of pure Wax,
His Dame and his two beauteous little Children,
    With Velvet on their backs.

Platters for each there were shin-shining,
    Of Silver many a pound,
And all of beaten Gold, three brimming Goblets,
    Standing the table round.

The smell that rose up richly from the Baked Meats
    Came thinning amid the boughs,
And much that greedy Thief who snuffed the night air —
    His Hunger did arouse.

He watched them eating, drinking, laughing, talking,
  Busy with finger and spoon,
While three most cunning Fiddlers, clad in crimson,
  Played them a supper-tune.

And he waited in the tree-top like a Starling,
  Till the Moon was gotten low;
When all the windows in the walls were darkened,
  He softly in did go.

There Robin and his Dame in bed were sleeping,
  And his Children young and fair;
Only Robin's Hounds from their warm kennels
  Yelped as he climbed the stair.

All, all were sleeping, page and fiddler,
  Cook, scullion, free from care;
Only Robin's Stallions from their stables
  Neighed as he climbed the stair.

A wee wan light the Moon did shed him,
  Hanging above the sea,
And he counted into his bag (of beaten Silver)
  Platters thirty-three.

Of Spoons three score; of jolly golden Goblets
  He stowed in four save one,
And six fine three-branched Cupid Candlesticks,
  Before his work was done.

Nine bulging bags of Money in a cupboard,
  Two Snuffers and a Dish
He found, the last all studded with great Garnets
  And shapen like a Fish.

Then tiptoe up he stole into a Chamber,
  Where on Tasselled Pillows lay
Robin and his Dame in dreaming slumber,
  Tired with the summer's day.

That Thief he mimbled round him in the gloaming,
    Their Treasures for to spy,
Combs, Brooches, Chains, and Rings, and Pins and Buckles
    All higgledy piggle-dy.

A Watch shaped in the shape of a flat Apple
    In purest Crystal set,
He lifted from the hook where it was ticking
    And crammed in his Pochette.

He heaped the pretty Baubles on the table,
    Trinkets, Knick-knackerie,
Pearls, Diamonds, Sapphires, Topazes, and Opals —
    All in his bag put he.

And there in night's pale Gloom was Robin dreaming
    He was hunting the mountain Bear,
While his Dame in peaceful slumber in no wise heeded
    A greedy Thief was there.

And that ravenous Thief he climbed up even higher,
    Till into a chamber small
He crept where lay poor Robin's beauteous Children,
    Lovelier in sleep withal.

Oh, fairer was their Hair than Gold of Goblet,
    'Yond Silver their Cheeks did shine,
And their little hands that lay upon the linen
    Made that Thief's hard heart to pine.

But though a moment there his hard heart faltered,
    Eftsoones he took the twain,
Slipped them into his Bag with all his Plunder,
    And softly stole down again.

Spoon, Platter, Goblet, Ducats, Dishes, Trinkets,
    And those two Children dear,
A-quaking in the clinking and the clanking,
    And half bemused with fear,

He carried down the stairs into the Courtyard,
    But there he made no stay,
He just tied up his Garters, took a deep breath,
    And ran like the wind away.

Past Forest, River, Mountain, River, Forest —
    He coursed the whole night through,
Till morning found him come into a Country,
    Where none his bad face knew.

Past Mountain, River, Forest, River, Mountain —
    That Thief's lean shanks sped on,
Till Evening found him knocking at a Dark House,
    His breath now well-nigh gone.

There came a little maid and asked his Business;
    A Cobbler dwelt within;
And though she much disliked the Bag he carried,
    She led the Bad Man in.

He bargained with the Cobbler for a lodging
    And soft laid down his Sack —
In the Dead of Night with none to spy or listen —
    From off his weary Back.

And he taught the little Chicks to call him Father,
    And he sold his stolen Pelf,
And bought a Palace, Horses, Slaves, and Peacocks,
    To ease his wicked self.

And though the Children never really loved him,
    He was rich past all belief;
While Robin and his Dame o'er Delf and Pewter
    Spent all their Days in Grief.

Grim

Beside the blaze, as of forty fires,
Giant Grim doth sit,
Roasting a thick-woolled mountain sheep
Upon an iron spit.
Above him wheels the winter sky,
Beneath him, fathoms deep,
Lies hidden in the valley mists
A village fast asleep —
Save for one restive hungry dog
That, snuffing towards the height,
Smells Grim's broiled supper-meat, and spies
His watch-fire twinkling bright.

The Unfinished Dream

Rare-sweet the air in that unimagined country —
    My spirit had wandered far
From its weary body close-enwrapt in slumber
    Where its home and earth-friends are;

A milk-like air — and of light all abundance;
    And there a river clear
Painting the scene like a picture on its bosom,
    Green foliage drifting near.

No sign of life I saw, as I pressed onward,
    Fish, nor beast, nor bird,
Till I came to a hill clothed in flowers to its summit,
    Then shrill small voices I heard.

And I saw from concealment a company of elf-folk
  With faces strangely fair,
Talking their unearthly scattered talk together,
  A bind of green-grasses in their hair,

Marvellously gentle, feater far than children,
  In gesture, mien and speech,
Hastening onward in translucent shafts of sunshine,
  And gossiping each with each.

Straw-light their locks, on neck and shoulder falling,
  Faint of almond the silks they wore,
Spun not of worm, but as if inwoven of moonbeams
  And foam on rock-bound shore;

Like lank-legged grasshoppers in June-tide meadows,
  Amalillios of the day,
Hungrily gazed upon by me — a stranger,
  In unknown regions astray.

Yet, happy beyond words, I marked their sunlit faces,
  Stealing soft enchantment from their eyes,
Tears in my own confusing their small image,
  Hearkening their bead-like cries.

They passed me, unseeing, a waft of flocking linnets;
  Sadly I fared on my way;
And came in my dream to a dreamlike habitation,
  Close-shut, festooned, and grey.

Pausing, I gazed at the porch dust-still, vine-wreathèd,
  Worn the stone steps thereto,
Mute hung its bell, whence a stony head looked downward,
  Grey 'gainst the sky's pale-blue —

  Strange to me: strange. . . .

V

The Last Coachload

To Colin

Crashed through the woods that lumbering Coach. The dust
Of flinted roads bepowdering felloe and hood.
Its gay paint cracked, its axles red with rust,
It lunged, lurched, toppled through a solitude

Of whispering boughs, and feathery, nid-nod grass.
Plodded the fetlocked horses. Glum and mum,
Its ancient Coachman recked not where he was,
Nor into what strange haunt his wheels were come.

Crumbling the leather of his dangling reins;
Worn to a cow's tuft his stumped, idle whip;
Sharp eyes of beast and bird in the trees' green lanes
Gleamed out like stars above a derelict ship.

'Old Father Time — Time — Time!' jeered twittering throat.
A squirrel capered on the leader's rump,
Slithered a weasel, peered a thief-like stoat,
In sandy warren beat on the coney's thump.

Mute as a mammet in his saddle sate
The hunched Postilion, clad in magpie trim;
The bright flies buzzed around his hairless pate;
Yaffle and jay squawked mockery at him.

Yet marvellous peace and amity breathed there.
Tranquil the labyrinths of this sundown wood.
Musking its chaces, bloomed the brier-rose fair;
Spellbound as if in trance the pine-trees stood.

D
97

Through moss and pebbled rut the wheels rasped on;
That Ancient drowsing on his box. And still
The bracken track with glazing sunbeams shone;
Laboured the horses, straining at the hill. . . .

But now — a verdurous height with eve-shade sweet;
Far, far to West the Delectable Mountains glowed.
Above, Night's canopy; at the horses' feet
A sea-like honied waste of flowers flowed.

There fell a pause of utter quiet. And —
Out from one murky window glanced an eye,
Stole from the other a lean, groping hand,
The padded door swung open with a sigh.

And — *Exeunt Omnes!* None to ask the fare —
A myriad human Odds in a last release
Leap out incontinent, snuff the incensed air;
A myriad parched-up voices whisper, 'Peace.'

On, on, and on — a stream, a flood, they flow.
O wondrous vale of jocund buds and bells!
Like vanishing smoke the rainbow legions glow,
Yet still the enravished concourse sweeps and swells.

All journeying done. Rest now from lash and spur —
Laughing and weeping, shoulder and elbow — 'twould seem
That Coach capacious all Infinity were,
And these the fabulous figments of a dream.

Mad for escape; frenzied each breathless mote,
Lest arouse the Old Enemy from his death-still swoon,
Lest crack that whip again — they fly, they float,
Scamper, breathe — 'Paradise!', abscond, are gone. . . .

The Listeners

'Is there anybody there?' said the Traveller,
  Knocking on the moonlit door;
And his horse in the silence champed the grasses
  Of the forest's ferny floor:
And a bird flew up out of the turret,
  Above the Traveller's head:
And he smote upon the door again a second time;
  'Is there anybody there?' he said.
But no one descended to the Traveller;
  No head from the leaf-fringed sill
Leaned over and looked into his grey eyes,
  Where he stood perplexed and still.
But only a host of phantom listeners
  That dwelt in the lone house then
Stood listening in the quiet of the moonlight
  To that voice from the world of men:
Stood thronging the faint moonbeams on the dark stair,
  That goes down to the empty hall,
Hearkening in an air stirred and shaken
  By the lonely Traveller's call.
And he felt in his heart their strangeness,
  Their stillness answering his cry,
While his horse moved, cropping the dark turf,
  'Neath the starred and leafy sky;
For he suddenly smote on the door, even
  Louder, and lifted his head: —
'Tell them I came, and no one answered,
  That I kept my word,' he said.
Never the least stir made the listeners,
  Though every word he spake
Fell echoing through the shadowiness of the still house
  From the one man left awake:
Ay, they heard his foot upon the stirrup,
  And the sound of iron on stone,
And how the silence surged softly backward,
  When the plunging hoofs were gone.

Which?

'What did you say?'
'I Nothing.' 'No? . . .
What was that sound?'
        'When?'
        'Then.'
'I do not know.'
'Whose eyes were those on us?'
        'Where?'
        'There.'
'No eyes I saw.'
'Speech, footfall, presence — how cold the night may be!'
'Phantom or fantasy, it's all one to *me*.'

All Hallowse'en

It was not with delight
That I heard in the dark
And the silence of night
The little dog bark.

It was not for delight
That his master had come
That so shrill rang his bark;
And at dawn, cold with rain,
That he yelped yet again:

But for fear, fury, fright
At the softness, the swiftness, the waft of the spright,
        Doomed to roam
        Through the gloom,
As the vague murk of night
Gave cold, grudging birth
To daybreak, on earth —

100

Wanning hillside and grove,
Once his lodgement and love:
    And now, poor soul,
    Hieing off home.

Solitude

When the high road
    Forks into a by-road,
And that drifts into a lane,
And the lane breaks into a bridle-path,
    A chace forgotten
    Still as death,
And green with the long night's rain;
Through a forest winding on and on,
Moss, and fern, and sun-bleached bone,
    Till only a trace remain;
And that dies out in a waste of stone
A bluff of cliff, vast, trackless, wild,
Blue with the harebell, undefiled;
Where silence enthralls the empty air,
Mute with a presence unearthly fair,
    And a path is sought
    In vain. . . .

It is then the Ocean
    Looms into sight,
A gulf enringed with a burning white,
A sea of sapphire, dazzling bright;
    And islands,
    Peaks of such beauty that
Bright danger seems to lie in wait,
Dread, disaster, boding fate;
And soul and sense are appalled thereat;
Though an Ariel music on the breeze
Thrills the mind with a lorn unease,
Cold with all mortal mysteries.

And every thorn,
And weed, and flower,
And every time-worn stone
A challenge cries on the trespasser:
Beware!
Thou art alone!

The Old Stone House

Nothing on the grey roof, nothing on the brown,
Only a little greening where the rain drips down;
Nobody at the window, nobody at the door,
Only a little hollow which a foot once wore;
But still I tread on tiptoe, still tiptoe on I go,
Past nettles, porch, and weedy well, for oh, I know
A friendless face is peering, and a clear still eye
Peeps closely through the casement as my step goes by.

The Spectre

In cloudy quiet of the day,
While thrush and robin perched mute on spray,
A spectre by the window sat,
        Brooding thereat.

He marked the greenness of the Spring,
Daffodil blowing, bird a-wing —
Yet dark the house the years had made
        Within that Shade.

Blinded the rooms wherein no foot falls.
Faded the portraits on the walls.
Reverberating, shakes the air
        A river there.

Coursing in flood, its infinite roars;
From pit to pit its water pours;
And he, with countenance unmoved,
      Hears cry: — 'Beloved,

'Oh, ere the day be utterly spent,
Return, return, from banishment.
The night thick-gathers. Weep a prayer
      For the true and fair!'

The Ghost

'Who knocks?' 'I, who was beautiful,
  Beyond all dreams to restore,
I, from the roots of the dark thorn am hither.
  And knock on the door.'

'Who speaks?' 'I — once was my speech
  Sweet as the bird's on the air,
When echo lurks by the waters to heed;
  'Tis I speak thee fair.'

'Dark is the hour!' 'Ay, and cold.'
  'Lone is my house.' 'Ah, but mine?'
'Sight, touch, lips, eyes yearned in vain.'
  'Long dead these to thine . . .'

Silence. Still faint on the porch
  Brake the flames of the stars.
In gloom groped a hope-wearied hand
  Over keys, bolts, and bars.

A face peered. All the grey night
  In chaos of vacancy shone;
Nought but vast sorrow was there —
  The sweet cheat gone.

Spake the fire-tinged bramble, bossed with gleaming fruit and
    blossoming,
    Gently serpentining in the air a blunted tongue : —
'Far too long these bones I hide have blackened in my covert here,
    Too long their noxious odour to my sweetness now hath clung.
Would they were gross clay, and their evil spell removed from me ;
    How much lovelier I, if my roots not thence had sprung.'

Breathed the wind of sundown, 'Ay, this haunt is long years sour
    to me ;
    But naught on earth that's human can my fancy free beguile.
Wings are mine far fleeter than the birds' that clip these branches ;
    Arabian rich the burden which for honeyed mile on mile
Is wafted on my bosom, hill to ocean, wood to valeland.
    Anathema on relics that my fragrances defile !'

Stirred a thousand frondlets and the willow tree replied to it : —
    'Sty and mixen, foetid pool, and carrion-shed — whose these?
Yet earth makes sweet the foulest ; naught — naught stays long
    unclean to her ;
    Thou, too, howe'er reluctant, art her servant, gliding Breeze.
Restrain thy fretting pudency ; in pity sigh for one I knew —
    The woman whose unburied bones in thornbrake take their
    ease.'

'*Urkkh :* when dark hath thicked to night,' croaked vermin toad
    that crouched near-by,
    'And the stars that mock in heaven unto midnight's cope have
    clomb,
When the shades of all the humans that in life were brutal foes to
    me
    Lift thready lamentation from the churchyard's rancid loam —
Return doth she in mortal guise 'gainst whom I bear no enmity,
    Foredoomed by fate this treacherous field for aye to haunt and
    roam.'

'Pictured once her image I,' sang sliding brook its rushes from,
  'That sallow face, and eyes that seemed to stare as if in dream,
Narrow shoulders, long lean hands, and hair like withered grass in
    hue,
  Pale lips drawn thwart with grieving in stars' silver mocking
    beam.
Once, too, I heard her story, but little I remember now,
  Though the blood that gave her power to suffer then imbrued
    my stream.'

Stony rock groaned forth its voice, 'No mirror featly shattered I,
  Blind I am by nature, but, I boast, not deaf or dumb,
Small truck I pay to Time's decay, nor mark what wounds black
    winter makes.
  Not mine to know what depths of snow have thawed and left
    me numb —
Since an eve when flowers had cast their seed, and evening cooled
    my brow again.
  And I echoed to a voice that whispered, "Loved one, I have
    come." '

Wafting through the woodland swept an owl from out the silent-
    ness,
  'Too wittoo woo,' she hooted. 'A human comes this way,
Gliding as on feathered heel, so tenuous that the thorns she skirts
  To eyes bright-glassed for glooms like mine show black beyond
    her grey.
A tryst she keeps. Beware, good friends, not mine day's mortal
    company,
  Hungry my brood for juicier fare,' she squawked, and plumed
    away.

Lone, in a shoal of milk-white cloud, bathed now the punctual
    fickle moon
  That nook of brook and willow, long unpolled, with silvery
    glare : —
'Unstilled yet tranquil Phantom, see, thou canst not hide thy form
    from me :

105

When last thy anguished body trod these meadows fresh and
    fair,
I, the ringing sand-dunes of the vast Sahara hoared with light:
    What secret calls thee from the shades; why hither dost thou
    fare?' . . .

Small beauty graced the spectre pondering mute beneath the
    willow-boughs
    O'er relics long grown noisome to the bramble and the breeze;
A hand upon her narrow breast, her head bent low in shadowiness;
    'I've come,' sighed voice like muted bell of nightbird in the
    trees,
'To tell again for all to hear, the wild remorse that suffers me,
    No single thought of rest or hope whereon to muse at ease.

'Self-slaughtered I, for one I loved, who could not give me love
    again,
    Uncounted now the Autumns since that twilight hour malign
When, insensate for escape from a hunger naught could satisfy,
    I vowed to God no more would I in torment live and pine.
Alas! He turned His face away, and woeful penance laid on me —
    That every night make tryst must I till life my love resign.'

Furtive fell the anxious glance she cast that dreadful hiding-
    place;
    Strangely still and muted ceased the tones in which she spake.
Shadow filled her vacant place. The moon withdrew in cloud
    again.
    Hushed the ripples grieving to the pebbles in their wake.
'Thus her *tale!*' quoth sod to sod. 'Not ours, good friends, to
    challenge it;
    Though her blood still cries for vengence on her murderer from
    this brake!'

The Forest

'Death-cold is this house. Beasts prowl at its threshold;
A forest of darkness besieges its gate,
Where lurks the lynx, Envy; the leopard named
    Malice;
And a gaunt, famished wolf, padding softly, called
    Hate.

'So when that fair She, there — slant eyes and slim
    shoulders,
Voice stealthy with venom — our solitude shares,
I sit with my sewing away from the window,
Since it's thence that the wild cat called Jealousy glares.

'But supposing ajar were that door — she alone here?
And my whisper the black stagnant forest lipped
    through? . . .
No, she sips of my wine; breaks bread; has no notion
It is I, the despised one, those bolts might undo.'

The Feckless Dinner-Party

'Who are we waiting for?' '*Soup* burnt?' . . . Eight —
  'Only the tiniest party. — Us!'
'Darling! Divine!' 'Ten minutes late — '
  'And my digest — ' 'I'm *ravenous*!'

' "Toomes"?' — 'Oh, he's new.' 'Looks crazed, I guess.'
' "Married" — *Again!*' 'Well; more or less!'

'Dinner is *served!*' ' "Dinner is served" !'
  'Is served?' 'Is served.' 'Ah, yes.'

'Dear Mr. Prout, will you take down
  The Lilith in leaf-green by the fire?
Blanche Ogleton? . . .' 'How coy a frown! —
  Hasn't she borrowed *Eve's* attire?'
'Morose Old Adam!' 'Charmed — I vow.'
  'Come then, and meet her now.'

'Now, Dr. Mallus — would you please? —
  Our daring poetess, Delia Seek?'
'The lady with the bony knees?'
  'And — *entre nous* — less song than beak.'
'Sharing her past with Simple Si — '
  '*Bare* facts! He'll blush!' 'Oh, fie!'

'And *you*, Sir Nathan — false but fair! —
  That fountain of wit, Aurora Pert.'
'More wit than It, poor dear! But there . . .'
  'Pitiless Pacha! *And* such a flirt!'
' "Flirt"! *Me?*' 'Who else?' 'You here. . . . Who can . . . ?'
  'In*corrigible* man!'

'And now, Mr. Simon — little me ! —
    Last and — ' 'By no means least !' 'Oh, come !
What naughty, naughty flattery !
    Honey! — I *hear* the creature hum !'
'Sweets for the sweet, *I* always say !'
    ' "Always"? . . . We're last. '*This* way?' . . .

'No, sir ; straight on, please.' 'I'd have vowed ! —
    I came the other . . .' 'It's queer ; I'm sure . . .'
'What frightful pictures !' 'Fiends !' 'The *crowd!*'
    'Such nudes !' 'I can't endure . . .'

'Yes, *there* they go.' 'Heavens ! *Are* we right?'
    'Follow up closer !' ' "Prout"? — sand-blind !'
'This endless . . .' 'Who's turned down the light?'
    'Keep calm ! They're close behind.'

'Oh ! Dr. Mallus ; what dismal stairs !'
    'I hate these old Victor . . .' 'Dry rot !'
'Darker and darker !' 'Fog !' 'The air's . . .'
    'Scarce breathable !' 'Hell !' '*What ?*'

'The banister's gone !' 'It's deep ; keep close !'
    'We're going down and down !' 'What fun !'
'Damp ! Why, my shoes . . .' 'It's slimy . . . Not *moss!*'
    'I'm freezing cold !' 'Let's run.'

'. . . Behind us. I'm giddy. . . .' 'The catacombs . . .'
    'That shout !' 'Who's there?' 'I'm *alone!*' 'Stand back !'
'She said, Lead . . .' 'Oh !' 'Where's Toomes?' '*Toomes!*'
        'TOOMES !'
    'Stifling !' 'My skull will crack !'

'Sir Nathan! *Ai!*' 'I *say! Toomes!* Prout!'
  'Where? Where?' ' "Our silks and fine array" . . .'
'She's mad.' 'I'm dying!' 'Oh, Let me *out!*'
  'My God! We've lost our way!' . . .

And now how sad-serene the abandoned house,
Whereon at dawn the spring-tide sunbeams beat;
And time's slow pace alone is ominous,
And naught but shadows of noonday therein meet;
Domestic microcosm, only a Trump could rouse:
And, pondering darkly, in the silent rooms,
He who misled them all — the butler, Toomes.

VI

Bitter Waters

In a dense wood, a drear wood,
   Dark water is flowing;
Deep, deep, beyond sounding,
   A flood ever flowing.

There harbours no wild bird,
   No wanderer stays there;
Wreathed in mist, sheds pale Ishtar
   Her sorrowful rays there.

Take thy net; cast thy line;
   Manna sweet be thy baiting;
Time's desolate ages
   Shall still find thee waiting

For quick fish to rise there,
   Or butterfly wooing,
Or flower's honeyed beauty,
   Or wood-pigeon cooing.

Inland wellsprings are sweet;
   But to lips, parched and dry,
Salt, salt is the savour
   Of these; faint their sigh.

Bitter Babylon's waters.
   Zion, distant and fair.
We hanged up our harps
   On the trees that are there.

In Disgrace

The fear-dulled eyes in the pallid face
Stared at the darkening window-pane;
Sullen, derided, in disgrace —
They watched night narrowing in again:
Far-away shoutings; a furtive wind
Which a keyhole had found; a star aloof;
A heart at war with a blunted mind;
   And a spout dripping rain from the roof: —

Drip — drip . . . till the light is gone;
But a heart not so hard as a stone.

The Dead Jay

A witless, pert, bedizened fop,
   Man scoffs, resembles you:
Fate levels all — voice harsh or sweet —
   Ringing the woodlands through:
But, O, poor hapless bird, that broken death-stilled wing,
   That miracle of blue!

Drugged

Inert in his chair,
In a candle's guttering glow;
His bottle empty,
His fire sunk low;
With drug-sealed lids shut fast,
Unsated mouth ajar,
This darkened phantasm walks
Where nightmares are:

In a frenzy of life and light,
Crisscross — a menacing throng —
They gibe, they squeal at the stranger,
Jostling along,
Their faces cadaverous grey:
While on high from an attic stare
Horrors, in beauty apparelled,
Down the dark air.

A stream gurgles over its stones,
The chambers within are a-fire.
Stumble his shadowy feet
Through shine, through mire;
And the flames leap higher.
In vain yelps the wainscot mouse;
In vain beats the hour;
Vacant, his body must drowse
Until daybreak flower —

Staining these walls with its rose,
And the draughts of the morning shall stir
Cold on cold brow, cold hands.
And the wanderer
Back to flesh house must return.
Lone soul — in horror to see,
Than dream more meagre and awful,
Reality.

Echo

'Who called?' I said, and the words
  Through the whispering glades,
Hither, thither, baffled the birds —
  'Who called? Who called?'

The leafy boughs on high
  Hissed in the sun;
The dark air carried my cry
  Faintingly on:

Eyes in the green, in the shade,
  In the motionless brake,
Voices that said what I said,
  For mockery's sake:

'Who cares?' I bawled through my tears;
  The wind fell low:
In the silence, 'Who cares? Who cares?'
  Wailed to and fro.

The Mourner

'Nothing for him on earth went right.
  A destined outcast he,
A bastard hustled out of sight,
  A stark epitome
Of all betokening Fortune's spite,
  And human apathy.

'There lurked beyond his vacant eyes
  A soul in mute eclipse —
A sea named *Nothing*, harbourless,
  Sans wind, sans sun, sans ships;
Of will, of mind, of eagerness
  No trace in those loose lips.

'His bridgeless nose, his toneless cry,
    His clumsy hands, his gait,
Sheer satire of humanity,
    Proclaimed a loon's estate;
"Made in God's image" — ay, meant to be:
    This mommet, scorned of Fate.

'He was not even monstrous enough
    To extort a schoolboy's jeers;
Too tame to cause a fool to scoff,
    Or incite a woman's fears.
He lived beyond the reach of love —
        For thirty years!'

' "Beyond the reach of love"! You say?
    Whence then these scalding tears?'

The Fat Woman

Massed in her creaseless black,
She sits; vast and serene;
Light — on glossed hair, large knees,
Huge bust — a-sheen.

A smile lurks deep in her eyes,
Thick-lidded, motionless, pale,
Taunting a world grown old,
Faded, and stale.

Enormous those childless breasts:
God in His pity knows
Why, in her bodice stuck,
Reeks a mock rose.

The Bottle

Of green and hexagonal glass,
    With sharp, fluted sides —
Vaguely transparent these walls,
    Wherein motionless hides
A simple so potent it can
    To oblivion lull
The weary, the racked, the bereaved,
    The miserable.

Flowers in silent desire
    Their life-breath exhale —
Self-heal, hellebore, aconite,
    Chamomile, dwale:
Sharing the same gentle heavens,
    The sun's heat and light,
And, in the dust at their roots,
    The same shallow night.

Each its own livelihood hath,
    Shape, pattern, hue;
Age on to age unto these
    Keeping steadfastly true;
And, musing amid them, there moves
    A stranger, named Man,
Who of their ichor distils
    What virtue he can;

Plucks them ere seed-time to blazon
His house with their radiant dyes;
Prisons their attar in wax;
Candies their petals; denies
Them freedom to breed in their wont;
Buds, fecundates, grafts them at will;
And with cunningest leechcraft compels
    Their good to his ill.

Intrigue fantastic as this
    Where shall we find?
Mute in their beauty they serve him,
    Body and mind.
And one — but a weed in his wheat —
    Is the poppy — frail, pallid, whose juice
With its saplike and opiate fume
    Strange dreams will induce

Of wonder and horror. And none
    Can silence the soul,
Wearied of self and of life,
    Earth's darkness and dole,

More secretly, deeply . . . But finally? —
    Waste not thy breath;
The words that are scrawled on this phial
    Have for synonym, *death* —

Wicket out into the dark
    That swings but one way;
Infinite hush in an ocean of silence
    Aeons away —
Thou forsaken! — even thou! —
    The dread good-bye;
The abandoned, the thronged, the watched,
    the unshared —
    Awaiting me — I !

De Profundis

The metallic weight of iron;
The glaze of glass;
The inflammability of wood . . .

You will not be cold there;
You will not wish to see your face in a mirror;
There will be no heaviness,
Since you will not be able to lift a finger.

There will be company, but they will not heed you;
Yours will be a journey only of two paces
Into view of the stars again; but you will not make
    it.

There will be no recognition;
No one, who should see you, will say —
Throughout the uncountable hours —

'Why . . . the last time we met, I brought you some
        flowers!'

VII

The Accompaniment
[FOR A WOODCUT]

The man in the hat (whom you see in the picture)
    Mused softly one evening: 'I sit in this copse,
And the birds warble sweetly, for sweet is their nature;
    Yet they sing at haphazard: then — every one stops.

'Yes, as if at the lift of a baton or finger,
    The love-notes, *pu-wees,* and *too-witta-woos* cease,
Not a pause for applause, not a wing seems to linger,
    The forests fall mute — the whole world is at peace.

'I marvel. I marvel. For take, now, the linnet —
    That sociable haunter of charlock and gorse,
There is no sweeter throat with a melody in it,
    Still, *solo* he pipes as a matter of course!

'God forbid that with drum, cornet, triangle, cymbal,
    We should drown the wee cherubs. Assuredly not.
Still, my dear sister Jane on the harp is still nimble.
    Nor have I my old skill with the fiddle forgot . . .'

So now, as the sun in the West is declining,
    The twain to that hill hie, the birds hie there too;
Rings the plucking of harp-strings, the catgut's sweet pining,
    And a chorus *orchestral* ascends to the blue.

Besides which, a host of all small kinds of beasties,
    (They are shown on the cut, though Miss Jane's out of sight),
Having learned the harmonic a marvellous feast is,
    Troll out an *Amen* ere they part for the night.

'As I Went to the Well-Head'

As I went to the well-head
I heard a bird sing:
'Lie yonder, lie yonder
The Islands of Ling.

'Leagues o'er the water
Their shores are away,
In a darkness of stars,
And a foaming of spray.'

Ever

Ever, ever
Stir and shiver
The reeds and rushes
By the river:
Ever, ever,
As if in dream,
The lone moon's silver
Sleeks the stream.
What old sorrow,
What lost love,
Moon, reeds, rushes,
Dream you of?

The Fool's Song

Never, no never, listen too long,
To the chattering wind in the willows, the night bird's song.

'Tis sad in sooth to lie under the grass,
But none too gladsome to wake and grow cold where life's
    shadows pass.

Dumb the old Toll-Woman squats,
And, for every green copper battered and worn, doles out Nevers
    and Nots.

I know a Blind Man, too,
Who with a sharp ear listens and listens the whole world through.

Oh, sit we snug to our feast,
With platter and finger and spoon — and good victuals at least.

At the Keyhole

'Grill me some bones,' said the Cobbler,
    'Some bones, my pretty Sue;
I'm tired of my lonesome with heels and soles,
Springsides and uppers too;
A mouse in the wainscot is nibbling;
A wind in the keyhole drones;
And a sheet webbed over my candle, Susie, —
    Grill me some bones!'

'Grill me some bones,' said the Cobbler,
  'I sat at my tic-tac-to;
And a footstep came to my door and stopped,
And a hand groped to and fro;
And I peered up over my boot and last;
And my feet went cold as stones: —
I saw an eye at the keyhole, Susie! —
  Grill me some bones!'

Good-Bye

The last of last words spoken is, Good-bye —
The last dismantled flower in the weed-grown hedge,
The last thin rumour of a feeble bell far ringing,
The last blind rat to spurn the mildewed rye.

A hardening darkness glasses the haunted eye,
Shines into nothing the watcher's burnt-out candle,
Wreathes into scentless nothing the wasting incense,
Faints in the outer silence the hunting-cry.

Love of its muted music breathes no sigh,
Thought in her ivory tower gropes in her spinning,
Toss on in vain the whispering trees of Eden,
Last of all last words spoken is, Good-bye.

Misericordia

Misericordia!
Weep with me.
Waneth the dusk light;
Strange the tree;
In regions barbarous
Lost are we

I, Glycera,
And Silas here,
Who hath hid in sleep
His eyes from fear;
Wan-wide are mine
With a tear.

Misericordia!
Was I born
Only to pluck
Disaster's thorn?
Only to stray
Forlorn?

Dreamland

Annie has run to the mill dam,
Annie is down by the weir;
Who was it calling her name, then?
Nobody else to hear?
Cold the water, calm and deep,
Honey-sweet goldilocks half-asleep,
Where the green-grey willows weep,
Annie is down by the weir.

Waiting

'Waiting to . . .'
'Who is?'
'We are . . .
Was that the night-owl's cry?'
'I heard not. But see! the evening star;
And listen! — the ocean's solacing sigh.'
'You mean the surf at the harbour bar?'
'What did you say?'
'Oh, "waiting".'
' "Waiting?" —
Waiting what for?'
'To die.'

Old Shellover

'Come !' said Old Shellover.
'What?' says Creep.
'The horny old Gardener's fast asleep;
The fat cock Thrush
To his nest has gone;
And the dew shines bright
In the rising Moon;
Old Sallie Worm from her hole doth peep:
Come !' said Old Shellover.
'Ay !' said Creep.

The Song of Finis

At the edge of All the Ages
    A Knight sate on his steed,
His armour red and thin with rust,
    His soul from sorrow freed;
And he lifted up his visor
    From a face of skin and bone,
And his horse turned head and whinnied
    As the twain stood there alone.

No Bird above that steep of time
    Sang of a livelong quest;
No wind breathed,
        Rest:
'Lone for an end !' cried Knight to steed,
    Loosed an eager rein —
Charged with his challenge into Space:
    And quiet did quiet remain.

A Sign

How shall I know when the end of things is coming?
The dark swifts flitting, the drone-bees humming;
The fly on the window-pane bedazedly strumming;
Ice on the waterbrooks their clear chimes dumbing —
How shall I know that the end of things is coming?

The stars in their stations will shine glamorous in the black:
Emptiness, as ever, haunt the great Star Sack;
And Venus, proud and beautiful, go down to meet the day,
Pale in phosphorescence of the green sea spray —
How shall I know that the end of things is coming?

Head asleep on pillow; the peewits at their crying;
A strange face in dreams to my rapt phantasma sighing;
Silence beyond words of anguished passion;
Or stammering an answer in the tongue's cold fashion —
How shall I know that the end of things is coming?

Haply on strange roads I shall be, the moorland's peace around
    me;
Or counting up a fortune to which Destiny hath bound me;
Or — Vanity of Vanities — the honey of the Fair;
Or a greybeard, lost to memory, on the cobbles in my chair —
How shall I know that the end of things is coming?

The drummers will be drumming; the fiddlers at their thrum-
    ming;
Nuns at their beads; the mummers at their mumming;
Heaven's solemn Seraph stoopt weary o'er his summing;
The palsied fingers plucking, the way-worn feet numbing —
        And the end of things coming.

The Song of the Mad Prince

Who said, 'Peacock Pie'?
  The old King to the sparrow:
Who said, 'Crops are ripe'?
  Rust to the harrow:
Who said, 'Where sleeps she now?
  Where rests she now her head,
Bathed in eve's loveliness'? —
  That's what I said.

Who said, 'Ay, mum's the word';
  Sexton to willow:
Who said, 'Green dusk for dreams,
  Moss for a pillow'?
Who said, 'All Time's delight
  Hath she for narrow bed;
Life's troubled bubble broken'? —
  That's what I said.

VIII

The Ditch

Masked by that brilliant weed's deceitful green,
No glint of the dark water can be seen
Which, festering, slumbers, with this scum for screen.

It is as though a face, as false as fair,
Dared not, by smiling, show the evil there.

The Spotted Flycatcher

Gray on gray post, this silent little bird
Swoops on its prey — prey neither seen nor heard!
A click of bill; a flicker; and, back again!
Sighs Nature an *Alas*? Or merely, *Amen*?

Supper

Her pinched grey body,
In widow's fur,
Mousey daren't
From her wainscot stir;
Twitching nose,
And hollow ear,
She stoops and listens,
Stark with fear:

There, like a tiger,
Sleek and sly,
Grimalkin's crouched
With gloating eye,
Watching her door —
While over the crumbs
The dusk of deepening
Evening comes.

'Dry August Burned'

Dry August burned. A harvest hare
Limp on the kitchen table lay,
Its fur blood-blubbered, eyes astare,
While a small child that stood near by
Wept out her heart to see it there.

Sharp came the *clop* of hoofs, the clang
Of dangling chain, voices that rang.
Out like a leveret she ran,
To feast her glistening bird-clear eyes
On a team of field artillery,
Gay, to manœuvres, thudding by.
Spur and gun and limber plate
Flashed in the sun. Alert, elate,
Noble horses, foam at lip,
Harness, stirrup, holster, whip,
She watched the sun-tanned soldiery,
Till dust-white hedge had hidden away —
Its din into a rumour thinned —
The laughing, jolting, wild array:
And then — the wonder and tumult gone —
Stood nibbling a green leaf, alone,
Her dark eyes, dreaming. . . . She turned, and ran,
Elf-like, in to the house again.
The hare had vanished. . . . 'Mother,' she said,
Her tear-stained cheek now flushed with red,
'Please, may I go and see it skinned?'

Immanent

The drone of war-plane neared, and dimmed away;
The child, above high-tide mark, still toiled on.
Salt water welled the trench that in his play
He'd dug as moat for fort and garrison.

Lovely as Eros, and half-naked too,
He heaped dried beach-drift, kindled it, and lo!
A furious furnace roared, the sea winds blew . . .
Vengeance divine! And death to every foe!

Young god! — and not ev'n Nature eyed askance
The fire-doomed Empire of a myriad Ants.

Mr. Punch

A screech across the sands;
    A drum's dull thump;
Oh, wicked Mister Punch,
    Hook-nose and hump!
What corpse is this lies here? —
    An infant dear;
    And Judy listening
    In grief and fear,
    Knowing the Hangman
    With his rope draws near!

While lean Dog Toby yawns —
    Ruff, paws, and tail —
And now at starfish blinks,
    And now at pail.

A screech across the sands!
    That sullen thump!
Oh, wicked Mr. Punch,
    Belled cap, hook-nose
        and hump!

Hi!

Hi! handsome hunting man
Fire your little gun.
Bang! Now the animal
Is dead and dumb and done.
Nevermore to peep again, creep again, leap again,
Eat or sleep or drink again, Oh, what fun!

Tit For Tat

Have you been catching of fish, Tom Noddy?
   Have you snared a weeping hare?
Have you whistled, 'No Nunny,' and gunned a poor bunny,
   Or a blinded bird of the air?

Have you trod like a murderer through the green woods,
   Through the dewy deep dingles and glooms,
While every small creature screamed shrill to Dame Nature,
   'He comes — and he comes!'?

Wonder I very much do, Tom Noddy,
   If ever, when off you roam,
An Ogre from space will stoop a lean face
   And lug you home:

Lug you home over his fence, Tom Noddy,
   Of thorn-sticks nine yards high,
With your bent knees strung round his old iron gun
   And your head dan-dangling by:

And hang you up stiff on a hook, Tom Noddy,
   From a stone-cold pantry shelf,
Whence your eyes will glare in an empty stare,
   Till you are cooked yourself!

Not That Way

No, no. Guard thee. Get thee gone.
      Not that way.
See; the louring clouds glide on,
Skirting West to South; and see,
The green light under that sycamore tree —
      Not that way.

There the leaden trumpets blow,
      Solemn and slow.
There the everlasting walls
Frown above the waterfalls
      Silver and cold;
      Timelessly old:
      Not that way.

Not toward Death, who, stranger, fairer,
Than any siren turns his head —
Than sea-couched siren, arched with rainbows,
Where knell the waves of her ocean bed.
Alas, that beauty hangs her flowers
For lure of his demoniac powers:
Alas, that from these eyes should dart
Such piercing summons to thy heart;
That mine in frenzy of longing beats,
Still lusting for these gross deceits.
      Not that way!

Crazed

I know a pool where nightshade preens
Her poisonous fruitage in the moon;
Where the frail aspen her shadow leans
In midnight cold a-swoon.

I know a meadow flat with gold —
A million million burning flowers
In noon-sun's thirst their buds unfold
Beneath his blazing showers.

I saw a crazèd face, did I,
Stare from the lattice of a mill,
While the lank sails clacked idly by
High on the windy hill.

Mrs. Grundy

'Step very softly, sweet Quiet-foot,
Stumble not, whisper not, smile not:
By this dark ivy stoop cheek and brow.
Still even thy heart! What seest thou? . . .'

'High-coifed, broad-browed, aged, suave yet grim,
A large flat face, eyes keenly dim,
Staring at nothing — that's me! — and yet,
With a hate one could never, no, never forget . . .'

'This is my world, my garden, my home,
Hither my father bade mother to come
And bear me out of the dark into light,
And happy I was in her tender sight.

'And then, thou frail flower, she died and went,
Forgetting my pitiless banishment,
And that Old Woman — an Aunt — she said,
Came hither, lodged, fattened, and made her bed.

'Oh, yes, thou most blessed, from Monday to Sunday,
Has lived on me, preyed on me, Mrs. Grundy:
Called me "dear Nephew", on each of those chairs
Has gloated in righteousness, heard my prayers.

'Why didst thou dare the thorns of the grove,
Timidest trespasser, huntress of love?
Now thou hast peeped, and now dost know
What kind of creature is thine for foe.

'Not that she'll tear out thy innocent eyes,
Poison thy mouth with deviltries.
Watch thou, wait thou : soon will begin
The guile of a voice : hark ! . . .' 'Come in. Come in !'

Shadow

Beware! — breathes the faint evening wind?
Omen! — sighs dayspring's innocent air?
Stalks out from shadow, when drawn's the blind,
A warning Nothing, to shake the mind
    And touch the soul with care? —
    At midnight on thy stair?

Lurks there in every rose's sweet
A murderous whisper, *Fade must I ?*
Mutters the vagrant in the street,
Edging his way with anxious feet —
    Thou too art hastening by.
    Drones on the carrion fly?

Oh, climb thou down from fool's disdain;
Stoop thy cold lips to rag and sore;
Kiss the gaunt cheek while yet remains
Life's blood in it. Ay, hearken; again! —
  Thou art the thief, the murderer,
  The outcast at thy door.

In the Dock

Pallid, mis-shapen he stands. The World's grimed thumb,
Now hooked securely in his matted hair,
Has haled him struggling from his poisonous slum
And flung him, mute as fish, close-netted there.

His bloodless hands entalon that iron rail.
He gloats in beastlike trance. His settling eyes
From staring face to face rove on — and quail.
Justice for carrion pants; and these the flies.

Voice after voice in smooth impartial drone
Erects horrific in his darkening brain
A timber framework, where agape, alone
Bright life will kiss good-bye the cheek of Cain.

Sudden like wolf he cries; and sweats to see
When howls man's soul, it howls inaudibly.

Outcasts

There broods a hovel by a narrow way,
    Broken and overgrown;
Ay, though intemperately the sickle is thrust,
    Weeds seed, and flourish on.

Sunk in that garden is a broken well.
    Its waters hidden from sight —
Small comfort any bucket draws from thence,
    Ev'n though it dip all night.

A few lean fowls stalk, envious of the dust,
    A cock at midnight cries;
But from those fallow acres, near and far,
    No clarion replies.

The dog-day suns shower heat upon its thatch,
    Till sty and bog and dust
Breathe up a filthy odour to the heavens
    At every fitful gust.

The winter falls. With leaden nights; and days
    Frozen and parched and harsh;
Far in the valley-mist an idiot head
    Stoops o'er a sterile marsh.

His toil and travail are a fruitless gage
    Thrown down to Destiny;
His pleasure a besotted jest
    'Twixt sin and misery.

Hope in his eyes a phantasm in a tomb,
    Faith in his heart a flame
His masters dim with hatred and revolt,
    And sadden into shame.

He grunts and sweats, through the long drouth of noon,
    Broods, gazing into mud ;
Till, suddenly, upon his spade shall stream
    A light as bright as blood.

Then shall he rise against his naked door,
    Fronting a fading West,
The wrath of God within his glassy eyes,
    And ruddy on his breast.

An Old Cannon

Come, patient rust ;
Come, spider with thy loom,
Make of this enginery,
War's dateless tomb !

Frail bindweed, clamber, and cling,
And clog this motionless wheel ;
Upon its once hot throat
Hoar-frost, congeal !

O, may its thunder have won
A last surcease,
And its dark mouth of woe
Ever yet hollower grow
In praise of peace !

138

Napoleon

'What is the world, O soldiers?
        It is I:
I, this incessant snow,
        This northern sky;
Soldiers, this solitude
        Through which we go
                Is I.'

Swifts

(1943)

No; they are only birds — swifts, in the loft of the
        morning
Coursing, disporting, courting, in the pale-blue arc of
        the sky.
There is no venom for kin or for kind in their wild-
        winged archery,
Nor death in their innocent droppings as fleet in their
        mansions they fly;

Swooping, with flicker of pinion to couple, the loved
        with the loved one,
Never with malice or hate, in their vehement sallies
        through space.
Listen! that silken rustle, as they charge on their bee-
        hive houses,
Fashioned of dried-up mud daubed each in its chosen
        place.

Hunger — not fear — sharps the squawk of their feather-
    less nestlings;
From daybreak into the dark their circuitings will not
    cease:
How beautiful they! — and the feet on earth's heavenly
    mountains
Of him that bringeth good tidings, proclaimeth the
    gospel of peace!

IX

The Undercurrent

What, do you suppose, we're in this world for, sweet
   heart?
What — in this haunted, crazy, beautiful cage —
Keeps so many, like ourselves, poor pining human
   creatures,
As if from some assured, yet withholden heritage?
Keeps us lamenting beneath all our happy laughter,
Silence, dreams, hope for what may *not* come after,
While life wastes and withers, as it has for all mortals,
     Age on to age, on to age?

Strange it would be if the one simple secret
Were, that wisdom hides, as beauty hides in pebble,
   leaf and blade;
That a good beyond divining, if we knew but where to
   seek it,
Is awaiting revelation when — well, *Sesame* is said;
That what so frets and daunts us ev'n in all we love
   around us
Is the net of worldly custom which has penned us in and
   bound us;
     That — freed — our hearts would break for joy
      Arisen from the dead.

     Would 'break'? What do I say?
Might that secret, if divulged, all we value most betray!
     Make a dream of our real,
     A night of our day,
      That word said?

Oh, in case that be the answer, in case some stranger call us,
　　　　Or death in his stead ;
　　Sweet Nought, come away, come away !

Two Deep Clear Eyes

Two deep clear eyes,
Two ears, a mouth, a nose,
Ten supple fingers,
And ten nimble toes,
Two hands, two feet, two arms, two legs,
And a heart through which love's blessing flows.

Eyes bid ears
Hark :
Ears bid eyes
Mark :
Mouth bids nose
Smell :
Nose says to mouth,
I will :
Heart bids mind
Wonder :
Mind bids heart
Ponder.

Arms, hands, feet, legs,
Work, play, stand, walk;
And a jimp little tongue in a honey-sweet mouth,
With rows of teeth due North and South,
Does nothing but talk, talk, talk.

The Miracle

Who beckons the green ivy up
    Its solitary tower of stone?
What spirit lures the bindweed's cup
        Unfaltering on;
Calls even the starry lichen to climb
By agelong inches endless Time?

Who bids the hollyhock uplift
    Her rod of fast-sealed buds on high;
Fling wide her petals — silent, swift,
        Lovely to the sky?
Since as she kindled, so she will fade,
Flower above flower in squalor laid.

Ever the heavy billow rears
    All its sea-length in green, hushed wall;
But totters as the shore it nears,
        Foams to its fall;
Where was its mark? on what vain quest
Rose that great water from its rest? . . .

So creeps ambition on; so climb
    Man's vaunting thoughts. He, set on high,
Forgets his birth, small space, brief time,
        That he shall die;
Dreams blindly in his stagnant air;
Consumes his strength; strips himself bare;

Rejects delight, ease, pleasure, hope;
   Seeking in vain, but seeking yet,
Past earthly promise, earthly scope,
      On one aim set:
As if, like Chaucer's child, he thought
All but 'O *Alma!*' nought.

Incantation

Vervain . . . *basil* . . . *orison* —
Whisper their syllablings till all meaning is gone,
And sound all vestige loses of mere word. . . .
   'Tis then as if, in some far childhood heard,
A wild heart languished at the call of a bird,
Crying through ruinous windows, high and fair,
A secret incantation on the air:
     A language lost; which, when its accents cease,
     Breathes, voiceless, of a pre-Edenic peace.

All But Blind

All but blind
   In his chambered hole
Gropes for worms
   The four-clawed Mole.

All but blind
   In the evening sky
The hooded Bat
   Twirls softly by.

All but blind
  In the burning day
The Barn-Owl blunders
  On her way.

And blind as are
  These three to me,
So, blind to Some-One
  I must be.

All That's Past

Very old are the woods;
  And the buds that break
Out of the brier's boughs,
  When March winds wake,
So old with their beauty are —
  Oh, no man knows
Through what wild centuries
  Roves back the rose.

Very old are the brooks;
  And the rills that rise
Where snow sleeps cold beneath
  The azure skies
Sing such a history
  Of come and gone,
Their every drop is as wise
  As Solomon.

Very old are we men;
   Our dreams are tales
Told in dim Eden
   By Eve's nightingales;
We wake and whisper awhile,
   But, the day gone by,
Silence and sleep like fields
   Of amaranth lie.

'. . . All Gone . . .'

'Age takes in pitiless hands
All one loves most away;
Peace, joy, simplicity
Where then their inward stay?'

Or so, at least they say.

'Marvel of noontide light,
Of gradual break of day;
Dreams, visions of the night
Age withers all away.'

Yes, that is what they say.

'Wonder of winter snow,
Magic of wandering moon,
The starry hosts of heaven —
Come seventy, all are gone.

'Unhappy when alone,
Nowhere at peace to be;
Drowned the old self-sown eager thoughts
Constantly stirring in thee!' . . .

Extraordinary!
That's what they *say* to me!

Fare Well

When I lie where shades of darkness
Shall no more assail mine eyes,
Nor the rain make lamentation
    When the wind sighs;
How will fare the world whose wonder
Was the very proof of me?
Memory fades, must the remembered
    Perishing be?

Oh, when this my dust surrenders
Hand, foot, lip, to dust again,
May these loved and loving faces
    Please other men!
May the rusting harvest hedgerow
Still the Traveller's Joy entwine,
And as happy children gather
    Posies once mine.

Look thy last on all things lovely,
Every hour. Let no night
Seal thy sense in deathly slumber
    Till to delight
Thou have paid thy utmost blessing;
Since that all things thou wouldst praise
Beauty took from those who loved them
    In other days.

The Scribe

What lovely things
  Thy hand hath made :
The smooth-plumed bird
  In its emerald shade,
The seed of the grass,
  The speck of stone
Which the wayfaring ant
  Stirs — and hastes on !

Though I should sit
  By some tarn in thy hills,
Using its ink
  As the spirit wills
To write of Earth's wonders,
  Its live, willed things,
Flit would the ages
  On soundless wings

Ere unto Z
  My pen drew nigh ;
Leviathan told,
  And the honey-fly :
And still would remain
  My wit to try —
My worn reeds broken,
  The dark tarn dry,
All words forgotten —
  Thou, Lord, and I.

The Tomtit

Twilight had fallen, austere and grey,
The ashes of a wasted day,
When, tapping at the window-pane,
My visitor had come again,
To peck late supper at his ease —
A morsel of suspended cheese.

What ancient code, what Morse knew he —
This eager little mystery —
That, as I watched, from lamp-lit room,
Called on some inmate of my heart to come
Out of its shadows — filled me then
With love, delight, grief, pining, pain,
Scarce less than had he angel been?

Suppose, such countenance as that,
Inhuman, deathless, delicate,
Had gazed this winter moment in —
Eyes of an ardour and beauty no
Star, no Sirius could show!

Well, it were best for such as I
To shun direct divinity;
Yet not stay heedless when I heard
The tip-tap nothings of a tiny bird.

The Owl

What if to edge of dream,
When the spirit is come,
Shriek the hunting owl,
And summon it home —
To the fear-stirred heart
And the ancient dread
Of man, when cold root or stone
Pillowed roofless head?

Clangs not at last the hour
When roof shelters not;
And the ears are deaf,
And all fears forgot:
Since the spirit too far has fared
For summoning scream
Of any strange fowl on earth
To shatter its dream?

Second Childhood

What! heartsick still, grown old and grey
And second childhood on its way?
Still listening after ghosts that come
Only to find you far from home?
Not even your spectre there to tell
How loving, loved and lovable.

Still feigning that from outward things
Enduring consolation springs?
Still preening? Hopping perch to seed;
Mockery of song? As if your need
Were all in one small cage contained,
Nor hint of wilder bird remained.

In the long, arduous, bitter day
Scarce one half-audible Wellaway?
As though — alone — no strangled note
Rasped with affliction that dumb throat!
'Twill snap your very heart-strings soon;
Poor outcast, pining for the Moon! . . .

Lovely, she rides the quiet skies,
And glasses all grieved aching eyes;
She who ne'er yet, at any tide,
Revealed to earth her hidden side.
She who no night-bird ever taught
To sing, not what it must, but ought.

She sinks. The day breaks — mounts on high,
To gild with grace Man's bloodier dye,
His world in wreckage . . . Miriam, come:
Transfigure our hearts with trump and drum!
A harp, forsooth; and still to crave
For love, peace, joy! Beyond the grave?

X

Haunted

The rabbit in his burrow keeps
No guarded watch, in peace he sleeps;
The wolf that howls in challenging night
Cowers to her lair at morning light;
The simplest bird entwines a nest
Where she may lean her lovely breast,
Couched in the silence of the bough: —
But thou, O man, what rest hast thou?

Thy emptiest solitude can bring
Only a subtler questioning
In thy divided heart. Thy bed
Recalls at dawn what midnight said.
Seek how thou wilt to feign content,
Thy flaming ardour's quickly spent;
Soon thy last company is gone,
And leaves thee — with thyself — alone.

Pomp and great friends may hem thee round,
A thousand busy tasks be found;
Earth's thronging beauties may beguile
Thy longing lovesick heart awhile;
And pride, like clouds of sunset, spread
A changing glory round thy head;
But fade with all; and thou must come,
Hating thy journey, homeless, home.

Rave how thou wilt; unmoved, remote,
That inward presence slumbers not,
Frets out each secret from thy breast,
Gives thee no rally, pause, nor rest,

Scans close thy very thoughts, lest they
Should sap his patient power away;
Answers thy wrath with peace, thy cry
With tenderest taciturnity.

'Unheard Melodies'

A minstrel came singing in the way;
       And the children,
       Nothing saying,
       Gathered round him,
       From their playing,
In a bower of the shadowy may.

He stood in a loop of the green;
       And his fingers
       On the wires
       Feigned their heart's deep,
       Hidden desires
For a country that never was seen.

Like moonbeams in forests of trees,
       Like brook water
       Dropping sweetness,
       Like the wild hare
       In her fleetness,
Like the wings of the honey-sucking bees;

He drew each pure heart with his skill;
       With his beauty,
       And his azure,
       And his topaz,
       Gold for pleasure,
And his locks wet with dew of April.

Time sped; and night's shadows grew deep,
　　　　Came owl-hoot
　　　　From the thicket,
　　　　And the shrill note
　　　　Of the cricket
Called the children to silence and sleep. . . .

Strange, strange! though the minstrel is gone,
　　　　Yet that hawthorn
　　　　Fair and lonely
　　　　Stoops mutely
　　　　Waiting only
Till the clamour of noonday is done —

Until, in the faint skies of eve,
　　　　Far and sweetly,
　　　　Like a river,
　　　　Silver wires seem
　　　　Throbbing ever
As if echo in sorrow would grieve

In ears dulled with wrath and rebuke;
　　　　And like snowdrops
　　　　After winter,
　　　　Tired feet pause there,
　　　　And then enter
That bower by the midsummer brook.

O minstrel, keep thy tryst, sound thine airs
　　　　In a heart that
　　　　Oft forgets thee,
　　　　Scorns, reviles thee,
　　　　Tires, and frets thee
With the burden of silence it bears.

Faint Music

The meteor's arc of quiet; a voiceless rain;
The mist's mute communing with a stagnant moat;
The sigh of a flower that has neglected lain;
     That bell's unuttered note:

A hidden self rebels, its slumber broken;
Love secret as crystal forms within the womb;
The heart may as faithfully beat, the vow unspoken;
     All sounds to silence come.

The Last Chapter

I am living more alone now than I did;
This life tends inward, as the body ages;
And what is left of its strange book to read
Quickens in interest with the last few pages.

Problems abound. Its authorship? A sequel?
Its hero-villain, whose ways so little mend?
The plot? still dark. The style? a shade unequal.
And what of the dénouement? And, the end?

No, no, have done! Lay the thumbed thing aside;
Forget its horrors, folly, incitements, lies;
In silence and in solitude abide,
And con what yet may bless your inward eyes.

Pace, still, for pace with you, companion goes,
Though now, through dulled and inattentive ear,
No more — as when a child's — your sick heart knows
His infinite energy and beauty near.

His, too, a World, though viewless save in glimpse ;
He, too, a book of imagery bears ;
And, as your halting foot beside him limps,
Mark you whose badge and livery he wears.

The Remonstrance

I was at peace until you came
And set a careless mind aflame.
I lived in quiet; cold, content;
All longing in safe banishment,
Until your ghostly lips and eyes
    Made wisdom unwise.

Naught was in me to tempt your feet
To seek a lodging. Quite forgot
Lay the sweet solitude we two
In childhood used to wander through;
Time's cold had closed my heart about;
    And shut you out.

Well, and what then? . . . O vision grave,
Take all the little all I have !
Strip me of what in voiceless thought
Life's kept of life, unhoped, unsought ! —
Reverie and dream that memory must
    Hide deep in dust !

This only I say : — Though cold and bare
The haunted house you have chosen to share,
Still 'neath its walls the moonbeam goes
And trembles on the untended rose;
Still o'er its broken roof-tree rise
The starry arches of the skies;
And in your lightest word shall be
The thunder of an ebbing sea.

The Monologue

Alas, O Lovely One,
  Imprisoned here,
I tap; thou answerest not,
  I doubt, and fear.
Yet transparent as glass these walls,
  If thou lean near.

Last dusk, at those high bars
  There came, scarce-heard,
Claws, fluttering feathers,
  Of deluded bird —
With one shrill, scared, faint note
  The silence stirred.

Rests in that corner,
  In puff of dust, a straw —
Vision of harvest-fields
  I never saw,
Of strange green streams and hills,
  Forbidden by law.

These things I whisper,
  For I see — in mind —
Thy caged cheek whiten
  At the wail of wind,
That thin breast wasting; unto
  Woe resigned.

Take comfort, listen!
  Once we twain were free;
There was a Country —
  Lost the memory . . .
Lay thy cold brow on hand,
  And dream with me.

Awaits me torture;
  I have smelt their rack;
From spectral groaning wheel
  Have turned me back;
Thumbscrew and boot, and then —
  The yawning sack.

Lean closer, then!
  Lay palm on stony wall.
Let but thy ghost beneath
  Thine eyelids call:
'Courage, my brother!' Nought
  Can then appal.

Yet coward, coward am I,
  And drink I must
When clanks the pannikin
  With the longed-for crust;
Though heart within is sour
  With disgust.

Long hours there are,
  When mutely tapping — well,
Is it to Vacancy
  I these tidings tell?
Knock these numb fingers against
  An empty cell?

Nay, answer not.
  Let still more longing make
Thy presence sure to me,
  While in doubt I shake:
Be but my Faith in thee,
  For sanity's sake.

Lost World

Why, inward companion, are you so dark with
      anguish?
A trickle of rancid water that oozes and veers,
Picking its sluggish course through slag and refuse,
Down at length to the all-oblivious ocean —
What else were apt comparison for your tears?

But no : not of me are you grieving, nor for me either ;
Though I, it seems, am the dungeon in which you dwell,
Derelict, drear, with skeleton arms to heaven,
Wheels broken, abandoned, greenless, vacant, silent ;
      Nought living that eye can tell.

Blame any man might the world wherein he harbours,
Washing his hands like Pilate, of all its woes ;
And yet in deadly revolt at its evil and horror,
That has brought pure life to this pass, smit through
          with sorrow,
Since he was its infamous wrecker full well he knows.

Not yours the blame. Why trouble me then with your
      presence?
Linger no instant, most Beautiful, in this hell.
No touch of time has marred your immutable visage ;
Eros himself less radiant was in his dayspring ! —
Or nearer draw to your heartsick infidel !

The Quiet Enemy

Hearken! — now the hermit bee
Drones a quiet threnody;
Greening on the stagnant pool
The criss-cross light slants silken-cool;
In the venomed yew tree wings
Preen and flit. The linnet sings.

Gradually the brave sun
Droops to a day's journey done;
In the marshy flats abide
Mists to muffle midnight-tide.
Puffed within the belfry tower
Hungry owls drowse out their hour. . . .

Walk in beauty. Vaunt thy rose.
Flaunt thy transient loveliness.
Pace for pace with thee there goes
A shape that hath not come to bless.
I thine enemy? . . . Nay, nay.
I can only watch and wait
Patient treacherous time away,
Hold ajar the wicket gate.

XI

Winged Chariot

'Is every subject apt for rambling rhyme ? —
Some are intractable, and some sublime :
Only Eternity could master Time.

'As I sat by myself, I talked to myself,
And myself replied to me . . .'

'I, whom thou seest with horyloge in hande,
Am namèd Tyme, the lord of every howre. . . .'

. . . Why this absurd concern with clocks, my friend?
Watching Time waste will bring no more to spend,
Nor can retard the inevitable end.

Yet when, the old wide staircase climbed once more,
Your bag in hand, you attain its second floor,
Turn the Yale key in lock, sigh, open the door

And into these familiar rooms you slip —
Where even Silence pauses, finger on lip —
Three emulous metal tongues you wake from sleep.

Do they suffice you? No, you pause again.
And (as if mechanisms made by men
The Truth could tell) you search each face. And then,

Though every minute of your life's your own,
Though here you are 'master' and at ease, alone —
You ring up *TIM*; consult the telephone.

The *telephone* ! . . . Then, these precautions past,
Time made in Greenwich safely yours at last,
You set all three some fifteen minutes fast.

Psychopathist might guess the reason why
You indulge your wits in this mendacity.
Think *you* Man's 'enemy' is thus put by?

Think you so fleet a thing — that madcap hare
You daily waken from its nightlong lair —
Time, would consent such stratagems to share?

Or is it that you reassurance seek,
Deeming the Future will appear less bleak
Now that your clocks will 'go' a whole long week?

'..."O, it came ore my eare, like the sweet sound
That breathes upon a banke of Violets;
Stealing, and giving odours ..."'

If Time's a stream — and we are told it's so,
Its peace were shattered if you check its flow;
What Naiad then ev'n fingertip would show? —
Her imaged other-world in ruins? ... No:

Should once there haunt your too-attentive ear
A peevish pendulum, no more you'll hear
The soundless thunder of the distant weir

Which is Eternity. . . . Blest reverie:
When, from the serfdom of this world set free,
The self a moment rapt in peace may be;

Not void; but poised, serene, 'twixt praise and prayer,
Such as the flower-clocked woods and meadows share,
Lulled and fed only by day's light and air.

How punctual they! But to no *tic-toc* rune.
Theirs is an older code than 'May' and 'June';
As testifies 'Jack-go-to-bed-at-noon';
Airiest of ghosts, he goes to bed at noon!

'. . . Jocond day stands tiptoe on the mistie mountaine's top . . .'

Nimbused in his own song at dawn of day,
From earth's cold clods the skylark wings his way,
Into the sun-gilt crest of heaven to stray.

Housed in the dark of sleepy farms below,
At their own hour the cocks craned up to crow,
Their harems hearkening in obsequious row.

But wheel and barrel, ratchet, pawl, and spring?
Dear heart alive, how dull and dead a thing,
Compared with any creature on the wing,
Wherewith to measure even a glimpse of Spring.

Or, 'splitting seconds', to attempt to mete
The thrill with which a firefly's pinions beat.
Yes, or the languor, lingering and sweet,

When, lulled in the embraces of the sun,
The rose exults that her brief course is run
And heat-drowsed honey-bee has come; is gone.

Last night, at window idling, what saw I
Against the dusky summer greenery? —
Midges, a myriad, that up and down did fly,
Obedient to the breezes eddying by —
Sylphs scarcely of Time but of mere transiency:

An ovoid of intricate *winged* things, beautiful;
As on some sea-breeze morning, sunned and cool,
One may peer down upon a wavering shoal —
Like eddying weed in ebb-tide's lap and lull —
Of tiniest fish-fry in a rock-bound pool.

*'. . . Among which the elephant is the greatest and commeth nearest in wit and capacitie to
men . . .'*

The sage, slow elephant, night-scampering mouse,
Snug-wintering tortoise in his horny house,
To cark of frost and snow oblivious —
Share they, think you, our sense of time with us?

And that old sly close-fisted cockatoo —
Whose private life's a furtive *entre nous*,
What temporal lens did *his* round eye peer through
Whilst five kings reigned, and died — ere he died too?

Or, destined denizen of perpetual night,
She, of the termites? Bloated, teeming, white,
Huge and scarce motionable : yet her hosts' delight?

A-drowse in the ocean in an Arctic gale —
What clock ticks Vespers to the suckling whale?
And bids Aurora her heavenly face unveil?

'... *Whannè thet Aprille with his shourès sote*
The droghte of Marche hath percèd to the rote ...'

What jewelled repeater edged the cuckoo's wing,
Lovesick from Africa, to flit in Spring?
Only one ding-dong name to say and sing —
And dower our pipits with a fosterling?

Oh, what a tocsin has she for a tongue ;
How stealthy a craft to jilt her eggs and young,
And put them out to nurse their whole lives long ! —

This heiress of the primeval. How learned she
Time, season, mileage and the momentary? —
Two idle summers and a sundering sea ;
And all small honest birds for enemy.

If ev'n we share no thought with our own kind
But what with voice, face, words may be defined,
How shall these quicksands of Nature be divined?
How fathom the innate by means of mind?

Reason strives on to bridge the vague abyss
Sev'ring the human from the languageless,
Its countless kinds and spheres of consciousness.

Insight delights in heavenly mysteries
And loves the childish game of '*Well, now, guess!*'

'. . . Love is from the eye: but . . . more by glances than by full gazings; and so for envy and malice . . .'

See, now, that dwindling meteor in space
Which with its ruin illumed the night's hushed face:
As well *time* headlong Lucifer's disgrace!

And, fleeter ev'n than flickering lightning's glow,
Transfiguring hidden landscapes hushed below,
Imaged ideas through consciousness may flow:
Fruit raised from seed before ev'n leaf could show!

And feeling races thought. *One* stricken glance
At some, till then, scarce dreamed-of countenance —
The very soul's at gaze, as if in trance:

Poised like a condor in the Andean night,
When scarp and snowdrift, height to pinnacled height,
Transmute with wonder the first morning light.

So, in its innocence, love breaks upon the sight.

Hatred, dread, horror, too. As books relate: —
Thyestes when his own son's flesh he ate;
First stare at his iron cage of Bajazet;
And Œdipus — when parricide's his fate.

'. . . By which there sat an hory
Old agèd Sire, with hower-glasse in hand,
Hight Time . . .'

Dogged morn till bed-time by its dull demands,
The veriest numskull *clock*-cluck understands,
Eked out by solemn gestures of its hands:

A subtler language stirs in whispering sands:

That double ovoid of translucent glass;
The tiny corridor through which they pass,
Shaping a crescent cone where nothing was,

Which mounts in exquisite quiet as the eye
Watches its myriad molecules slip by;
While, not an inch above, as stealthily,

Those rocks minute might fall of waters be
Pouring themselves as imperturbably
Into the crystal of their central sea.

A tiny shallowing on the surface seen
Sinks to a crater where a plane has been.
Could mutability be more serene?

Invert the fragile frame; and yet again
Daydream will rear a castle built in Spain.
'Time' measured thus is dewfall to the brain.

Water-clock, clepsydra, candle-flame and daybreak.

So, out of morning mist earth's flowers arise,
Reflecting tintless daybreak in the skies;
And, soon, the whole calm orient with its dyes.

And even in bleak Winter one may go
Out of night's waking dreams and see the snow
In solemn glory on the fields below.

How happy he whose 'numbers' well as sweet,
Their rhythms in tacit concert with their feet,
And measure 'time', with no less hushed a beat. . . .

And clepsydra — the clock that Plato knew,
Tolling the varying hours each season through;
Oozing on, drop by drop, in liquid flow,
Its voice scarce audible, bell-like and low
As Juliet's communings with her Romeo.

More silent yet; pure solace to the sight —
The dwindling candle with her pensive light
Metes out the leaden watches of the night.
And, in that service, from herself takes flight.

'. . . The Sun's light when he unfolds it,
Depends on the Organ that beholds it . . .'

Ah, after vigil through the hours called small,
Earth's dumb nocturnal hush enshrouding all,
When dread insomnia has the soul in thrall,
To see that gentle flame greet sunrise on the wall!

Clocks fuss along, the lackeys of a spring;
Slaves of escapements; chime, but never sing:
Snow-soft as ghost-moth is *Time's* winnowing wing;
Though even to granite it some change must bring;

And to all else that's temporal. Which is yet
Nothing corrupt, but merely change. And that
On goal supreme — through change — its course may set.

And ev'n if ruin Nature's face betray,
Time was not cause thereof, but mere decay,
Slow as renewal, wending its wonted way.

'. . . One thinks the soul is air; another fire;
Another, blood diffused about the heart,
Another saith, the elements conspire.
And to her essence each doth give a part . . .'

When restless thought lulls low, as winds may cease
On dune and marram-grass, and there is peace,
The self becalmed may be by a loneliness

That pays no heed to time; and may attain
What Reason mocks at as the 'intense inane';
Though little one covet to come back again.

Sea-gulls home this way in the setting sun,
When — lowered lamp — his winter is begun.
He dyes their plumes with his vermilion,
As, in their idling squadrons, they wing on.

Under this roof, when, motionless and dense,
Silence beleaguers every nerve and sense,
Self-solitude is made the more intense.

Head turned on shoulder then, the straining ear
Dreads and yet conjures up the voice of Fear.
An inward sentry cries, 'Who's listening here?' . . .

Could fancy alone in this old thick-walled house,
When nothing stirs, not even a wainscot mouse,
Thus haunt mere matter with the ominous?
    And these misgivings rouse?

Midnight beyond that shutter broods. The rain
Its lully whispers in the towering Plane
Whose presence canopies my complete domain —

Whose every twig breathes freshness in the air,
And mottled boughs five-fathom tresses wear,
In May-time dangling like a Siren's hair.

'. . . In the Desarts of Africa, you shall meet oftentimes with fairies appearing in the
shape of men and women, but they vanish quite away like phantastical delusions . . .'

Phantoms draw nearer then of the unseen.
They pause in silence at the entering-in;
Eyes, raiment, wraithlike faces, vapour-thin —

Heeded perceptions of a secret mind
Less closely to the physical confined:
Like flowers in their beauty to the blind.

And every soul draws ever toward its own
Viewless associates as it journeys on;
Is never less alone than when alone.

When, then, I leave this haunt, as soon I may,
Will not some homesick relic of me stay —
Unseen, unheard? And while — what? . . . *Time*, away!?

'*Are they shadows that we see? . . .*'

Hearken the heart must if it seem to share
A rarer presence yet than light or air;
Visage serene, calm brows, and braided hair —

More real even than what imagining
Into the confines of the eye may bring;
Tranquil as seraph, with half-folded wing.

Would I her scholar were in poetry!
No toil in vain then. Nothing to weary me.
Alas, these halting rhymes — that cannot be.

Yet, when, a child, I was content to rove
The shingled beach that I was Crusoe of,
All that I learned there was akin to love.

The glass-clean billow toppling on the sand,
Sweet salt-tanged air, birds, rock-drift — eye, ear, hand;
All was a language love could understand.

'. . . *Those steps of stone . .* .'

Yet there was mystery too: those steps of stone —
In the green paddock where I played alone —
    Cracked, weed-grown,
Which often allured my hesitant footsteps down

171

To an old sun-stained key-holed door that stood,
The guardian of an inner solitude,
Whereon I longed but dreaded to intrude;
Peering and listening as quietly as I could.

There, as I knew, in brooding darkness lay
The waters of a reservoir. But why —
In deadly earnest, though I feigned, in play —
Used I to stone those doors; then run away,
Listening enthralled in the hot sunny day

To echo and rumour; and that distant sigh,
As if some friend profaned had made reply, —
   When merely a child was I?

'. . . Love is a malady apart, the sign
And astrolabe of mysteries Divine . . .'

Nor is this *love* a jewel in one plane.
It many facets has: mind, soul; joy, pain:
And even a child may to this truth attain.

Secret and marvel too the body is,
And exquisite means of earth's infrequent bliss;
But love foresees Love's everlastingness.

Had passion voice, why then the strange delight
Ev'n an hour may bring would pæans indite;
And, seeing no words these mercies could requite,
Age pines, in talk, to skirt the infinite;
As birds sing wildlier when it draws towards night.

'Whoe'er she be . . .'

She whom I vision many masks has worn,
Since, in this world, half-alien, I was born;
And every one has left me less forlorn.

172

And though pure solitude may be utmost grace,
And leagues from loneliness, a loved-one's face
Quadruples happiness in any place.

Time shared then's not time halved. Yet if it be
Spent in that loved one's fleeting company,
It flies even swiftlier than the caught set free.

Leaving an empty cage? . . . May heaven forbear!
Blank absence then would greet us everywhere —
A *wilderness*, called Time, bereft and bare
Be the slow tedium left however fair.

'. . . There mournful cypress grew in greatest store,
And trees of bitter gall, and Heben sad,
Dead-sleeping Poppy, and black Hellebore,
Cold coloquintida . . .'

However fair . . . . But cracked may be love's bells;
Mirage its lode-star, and disaster else;
As (countless cantos) this old fable tells: —

THE PALACE OF TIME

'A self-sick wanderer, in the leprous light
Of death-drear forest at the fall of night
Came out on no less derelict a sight: —

'Its walls slant-shadowed by the dwindling shine
Of day, a mansion — bleached, gaunt, saturnine,
With windows gaping 'gainst the evening green
As though by fire-flames charred their mullions had been

'It called to mind a dream he once was in. . . .

'That broken turret; fallen roof — were these
The prey of *age*? Weather's slow ravages?
Or sudden blasting stroke of destiny's?

173

'When what is beautiful is that no more,
Except as memory may its grace restore,
One's very heart stands listening at the door;

'And self-arraigned, the fatal charge must meet:
"Wilful neglect; betrayal; self-deceit."
And no defender left to answer it.

. . . And we watered our horses at the pool of Siloam . . .'

'What though once-Eden now is sour morass,
The abode of croaking frogs and venomous flies,
    Yet, which of us, alas,
Can not in his own visage darkly trace
    That blighted Seraph's face?

'And when, companionless, at night we fare,
Ascending our own private corkscrew stair,
Is't never Darkness that awaits us there? . . .

'Down the chill chace he paced . . . Where once the deer
Browsed in the dappling sun devoid of fear,
And supped the conduit's waters rippling clear;

'Where wooed the turtle-dove; and all dark long
Creatures nocturnal in its woods would throng,
And nightingales mock passion with their song;

'Now effigies, in guise of life, of stone —
Grief, woe, despair their broken faces on,
Some as though smiling — in the dusk-line shone.
All else seemed foundered in oblivion.

'And *Silence* mouldered there; aloof, alone.
Ev'n should the sun now shine and gild the tips
Of motionless cypresses in this wide ellipse,
His beams were shorn of power, as in eclipse.

'And formless shapes of rock that seemed to brood
On lost primordial secrets, crouched or stood,
Lifeless, yet menacing, margining the wood.

174

'... The lady rade, True Thomas ran,
Until they cam to a water wan;
O it was night and nae delight,
And Thomas wade aboon the kree.'

    'Yet no thing living showed, save where it seemed
    The stone-work of a dial vaguely gleamed;
    And there, though not asleep, one lay and dreamed.

    'Sickened with expectation, close he drew,
    The sun-warmed turf beneath his feet; and knew

It was dark night, and nae starlight,
And on they waded lang days three,
And they heard the roaring o a flood,
And Thomas a waefou man was he ...'

    Eyes glassy-cold as serpent's watched their thin lids through
        Lids fringed with gilt, and eyes of sleep-glazed blue.

    '*Palace of Time*, he had heard these ruins named;
    Once seat of Pride and Pomp, but long ill-famed,
    Since Pride had fallen, and venging fire had flamed.

'... Side by side, jarring no more,
Day and night side by side,
Each by a doorless door,
Motionless sit the bridegroom and bride
On the Dead-Sea-shore ....'

    'She, then, was Witchcraft, and on evil bent,
    Foe of the abandoned, lost, and malcontent,
    And doomed to ruin whithersoever they went?

    'The tarnished dial, its gnomon shorn away,
    Worn steps, now shattered, with cankering lichen grey,
    Told of phantasmal night, past hope of day.

    'A lunar dial? Astarte's wizardry?
    Secret, adored, cold, wanton in perfidy;
    The bygone haunt of ancient revelry?

'And he, this wanderer? What fate was his?' ...
So runs this ancient legend of dole and Dis;
Whereof no end's recorded beyond this.

'Like one who, victim of a malady,
Having its name, yet knows not what it be,
Seeking for light in some old dictionary,
Meets *caput mortuum*'s cold scrutiny ...'

*　　*　　*

'... *Feed apace then, greedy eyes, On the wonder you behold!* ...'

Love is life's liberty. 'Time' will snare remain
Until to peace of mind and heart we attain,
And paradise, whose source it was, come back again.

Inscrutable Nature in her own slow way
Seems even in labour to be half in play;
With hyssop in wall will dally a whole long summer's day.

She takes her time: and, the rich summer gone,
Through autumn mists and winter cold dreams on
Till, Phoenix-like, her beauty is re-won.

... *How often comes to memory — silly sooth! —*
That tiny bird I took to be a moth ...

Yes, and with what élan her creatures live,
How in their kinds, crafts, busyness they thrive!
The tribute lovely, wanton, odd they give

To all that nurtures them — the viewless air,
The Sun in dazzling bounty circling there,
Rivulet, bosoming hill and woodland fair.
Her faintest change each in its kind must share;

Unique, exultant beings of infinite zest,
Preying or preyed on, and supremely blest
In that by human cares they are unoppressed.

'. . . If things of Sight such heavens be,
What heavens are those we cannot see ? . . .'

How ponder quickly enough on what one sees
To realise this beauty's mutableness? —
Its range is one of infinite degrees.

Stir not your gaze, but let it so remain,
In all its quietude, in eye and brain;
Of its own nature it will soothe, and sain.

A plain wood panel will the whole long day
In light and shadow change with every ray.
No eye will *watch* that loveliness away.
Alas, that nothing can less briefly stay!

The moment is annulled — however dear —
Sooner than raptured tongue can utter, '*See, it's here!*'
Shrill from his midden-top whoops Chanticleer,
Scratches — and priceless gewgaws disappear.

Nor is some strangeness absent from the seen,
However usual, if there intervene
The unageing mind. Its hidden life has been
This edge of contrast to the day's routine.

Jasmine, and hyacinth, the briar rose
Steep with their presence a whole night; nor close:
Time with an infinite gentleness through them flows.

Fantastic growths there are too — flower and scent —
In earth's occult alembic strangely blent,
To some obscure decree obedient,
And as of sorcerous or divine descent.

Mist, dew and rainfall keep these trystings sweet,
And light, with ghosting shadow, dogs our feet;
Day in, day out, thrums on heart's secret beat,
Calmly refusing to conform with it.

While none of these then can 'pure time' bespeak,
Which every eager intellect should seek,
Each mind its time-piece has. And that's unique.

'... *Time was: Time is: Time is not* ...'

Time was: Time is: Time is not, runs the rune.
Hasten then. Seize that *is*, so soon begone.
As well subtract the music, keep the tune !

For no 'time' ever yet in storage lay,
Sun-ambered, weathered, sweet as new-mown hay,
Waiting mind's weaving — Rumpelstiltskin's way : —

Time 'real' ; time rare ; time wildfire-fleet ; time tame ;
Time telepathic, out of space, and aim ;
Time starry ; lunatic ; ice-bleached ; of flame ;
Dew-transient, yet immutably the same ;
Meek-mild as chickweed in a window-frame ;

Tardy as gathering dust in rock-hewn vault ;
Fickle as moon-flake in a mirror caught
At pause on some clear gem's scarce-visible fault ...

And how moves Time in triple darkness hid,
Where — mummied 'neath his coffered coverlid —
Sleeps on the Pharaoh in his pyramid :
Time disincarnate — and that sharp-nosed head?

Even though suave it seem as narded oil,
Fatal to beauty it is, and yet its foil.
It is of all things mortal the indifferent soil.

Eye scarce can tell where, the whole spectrum through,
Orange with yellow fuses, green with blue ;
So Time's degrees may no less diverse show,
Yet every variant be its fraction true.

Grey with their dust, cribbed in with facts and dates,
On foundered centuries the historian waits.
Ashes in balance, he sifts, weighs, meditates.

Unlike the astronomer in the heavens at play,
Through Time defunct, not Space, he elects to stray.
Stars of a magnitude his chosen prey,
He spends less leisure on its Milky Way,
Man's millions in its *Coalsack* stowed away.

Much he may look for which he is like to find;
And to its worst may be at length resigned:
'The follies, crimes, misfortunes of mankind.'

Transmuting facts into his truth, rejecting none,
Rapt in seclusion, he toils gravely on;
    Crypt, arch, pier, buttress, roof; and fickle moon —
    A noble structure when the building's done:
But of wild coarse sweet positive *life*, no breath — not one.

Yet, let disciple read him with delight —
In Time interred, a fellow-anchorite —
It is as though into the gloom of night
Scapegrace Aladdin chanced to come in sight,
And rubbed his lamp. . . . The change is infinite.
Shadows take bodies; blood begins to beat;

And through this inky ichor softly rills
The Jinnee's magic, and each cranny fills
With scene, thought, action, as the context wills;
And very life itself his record thrills.

So too in fane of Time's memorial stones —
In crisscross framework of poor human bones,
Isis, Baal, Ormuzd on their scaling thrones —
The scutcheons glimmer of the great Unknowns . . .
        And now — their withered *Once!*

. . . Sup humbly. All things compassed, near or far,
Are — for ourselves — but what we think they are:
The Web of Seeming holds us prisoner . . .

They touch us to the quick, these far events,
Looming beyond mere mortal instruments;
Omens of destiny, of Providence:
Their dust long fall'n, but not their influence.

But no rune's yet recalled Time's lost and gone —
Only its ghosts. And theirs is *dies non*.
All is in flux; nor stays, but changes on.
No sunrise hymns the self-same orison.

The unique's unique — assort it as we please;
Every oak's acorns will sprout differing trees.
So many lives, as many mysteries.

Nor do the morning stars together sing
One only *Laus* to *Alleluias*' ring,
When shout the sons of God before their King.

'. . . O tell me mair, young man, she said,
This does surprise me now;
What country hae ye come frae?
What pedigree are you? . . .'

Were moments seeds, we then therein might say
What hidden kind, hue, value, beauty lay,
Virtue and quality. But, these away,

Theirs only quantity, mere measurement,
Sans substance, pattern, form, shape, taste and scent —
Flimsier than bubble, and more transient.

Should, then a Stranger from another Sphere
Enquire, *'This Time, of which so much I hear?*
Light — dark; heat — cold; void — solid: these are clear;
But TIME? What is it? Show me some, Monsieur!'

What should we choose for semblance? A flake of snow?
A beach-brine bubble? A tiny shell or two?

Poised in the sun, pure diamond of dew?
Or whisper, *'Look! a* clock ! *Now watch Time flow;*
It's a Machine, *you see. It makes it go.'*

Bland face; sly jerking hands: staring he'd stay,
Dumbly astonished. And then turn, and say,
'Closer to Nothingness could nothing stray!
And now, pray, make Time flow the other *way!'*

'. . . O fairest flower no sooner blown than blasted,
Soft silken primerose, fading timelesslie . . .'

'Moments', like sun-discs on a rippled sea,
No heed paid to them merely cease to be,
Leaving no trace of their identity:

Mere litter stowed in Time's packed Lumber-Room —
Moth, spider, mildew, rust, star-raftered gloom;
Vast as moon-crater, silent as the tomb,
Not even a death-watch for a pendulum.

But mark Self summing up what's really his —
Glimpses of childhood, friendship, bygone bliss
Those fumbling fingers, that impassioned kiss !
Dear beyond words are relics such as these.

And who, in his dark hours, dulled, overcast —
At envy, hatred, malice, cant aghast —
Would not abscond a while from this worn temporal waste;
Into another world of being haste,
And, maybe, meet the idolised at last?
Chaucer? Keats? Marvell? Wyatt? Drayton? — Oh
Any long-lov'd and true enthusiast !

Lost in that company the spirit may range
A rarer, deeper, closer interchange
In the imagination, rich and strange —
A Mariana in a moated grange.

At shut of dusk, 'neath timbered roof, worn stone,
Dark at the window-glass, and all life gone,
In hush of falling dust and mouldering bone,

Inward, still inward let the round ear lean ! . . .
Time's not of moments made. It's hidden in
Some nameless stuff that oozes in between. . . .

'. . . "I stand like one
That long hath ta'en a sweet and golden dream,
I am angry with myself now that I wake" . . .'

Yet, friend, (once more), when you are here again,
Do you *possess* this quiet? The Silence drain?
Give thanks for boons withheld from other men?
A Paternoster breathe — and then count ten?

No, like some light-o'-love, away you chase
Straight to that *chit-chat* in the china case
You bought in Woodbridge — 'Fitz's' native place.
Then comes 'Susanna', with her prim round face;

Next your much-prized old dial, inlaid with brass,
Sun-pendulum'd in gilt. And next. . . .
                                        Alas,
Still will the hours for you melt much too fast !

Not for the world that I would mock at what
Have 'timed' the countless godsends of my lot;
And still might miss, most earthly things forgot.

'. . . Keeping time, time, time
To a sort of runic rhyme . . .!'

> Even as 'child of Paules', when brood I would
> At thunder of its bell — Night : Solitude —
> (And slow-coach was I always, doomed to plod),
> I must have fallen in love with clocks for good.
>
> Tompion, Bréguet, Knibb, Ellicot, Cole, Quare,
> How featly chime the names of those who were
> Masters in this sweet art ; famed everywhere :
> Timepiece-artificers beyond compare.
> And each of sovereign Harrison the heir,
>> With his supreme chronometer.
>
> Bell-tinkling *watch*-craft too, tiny as bees,
> Set bezel-wise, may match great clocks with ease —
> And, no less punctually, the Pleiades.
>
> And should you wish to meditate ; then, where
> A grandpaternal timepiece crowns the stair,
> Pause as you go to bed ; to listen ; and share
> The unhastening monologue it ponders there.

'. . . But at my back I alwaies hear
Times winged Charriot drawing near . . .'

> To Julius and Gregory be praise,
> Who bade the Calendar amend its ways.
> But when from such dull durance fancy strays —
> How beautiful is the procession of the days.
>
> With each cold clear pure dawning to perceive
> The Sun's edge earlier ; and, at fall of eve,
> When the last thrush his song is loth to leave,
> To mark its latening, however brief !

183

Nor is the marvel of his burning rose,
Bronze, saffron, azure, discontinuous;
He takes his splendour with him as he goes.

So thought the poet, Fabre d'Églantine,
(When his sweet France had licked the platter clean).
Brumaire . . . . Nivôse . . . . Vendémiaire — things *seen*
In Terra's tilt, from virgin white to green:

Snow . . . . Rain . . . . Wind . . . . Bud . . . Flower . . . . Grape
    make richer sense
Than our pastiche of dead-alive events —
Janus to Juno, and December thence.

Sick unto death must Woden be of Thor;
Deaf Saturn yells at Frig, '*We have met before!* . . .'
Sun unto Moon, '*Would God weeks were no more;*
Or that to Man He would his wits restore!' . . .

'. . . *And yonder al before us lye*
Desarts of vast Eternity . . .'

Still: dangling keys 'twixt clumsy finger and thumb,
You bustle your punctual way from room to room,
And into senseless tongues transform the dumb.

You wind the docile things — run-down or not;
You set them fast, as cautious mortals ought;
And are at once in TIM's sly coggery caught.

Yet hopes, joys, prayers will tell much more that is
In this strange world of ours of bale and bliss.
Ev'n specks of sand secrete eternities:
Sit down then; listen to their confidences.

Think you, indeed, benumbed by grief or pain,
Or lost in some dread labyrinth of the brain,
An earth-bound clock will set you free again?

Why pause not *now*? To ponder, unoppressed?
The halcyon come again. And in your breast
The brief Elysium of a soul at rest?

'. . . *As that fair flower Adonis, which we call an anemone flourisheth but one month . . . .*'

An opening flower, night's furthest nebulae
In mind supreme must be contemporary.
In one same moment they might cease to be.

And that faint eastern star — 'light-years' gone by
Its beams have ranged which pierce the evening sky,
To find their haven in a human eye;
On human heart to shed tranquillity.

And though with his ingenious Optick Glass
The mind of man may map the wastes of Space,
Thence he may yet return in joy to trace
The light of welcome in a human face.

Merely material things hark back again
To their unknown, unknowable origin;
As, to death-darkening gaze, the world of men.

Those rocks green-capped, round which the sea-mews whine,
Reared up aloft, wide-gullied from the land,
Are no more stable in the wash of Time
Than lost enchanted palace in the sand.

Sun-bleached, slim, delicate bones of wings at rest,
And whispering thrift that trembles in the blast
Tell of the transiency of earthly dust
To which even adamant must return at last.

There falls a night, of myriads gone by;
A starless tempest raves; the wildering sea
Storms in. And daybreak lifts a heavy eye
For what has gane its gaite, and ceased to be.

So, to day's eye, destruction shows — void space
Where towered massive majesty and grace,
Coped by the foam-flowers of sea-wilderness.

'. . . So did this noble Empire waste,
Sunk by degrees from glories past . . .'

Engirdling the great World these waters flow,
To charred wan moon obeisant, to and fro.
But swang she nearer? . . . Chaos and overthrow:
Which of our marvels then were left for show

Of all Man's pomp and power? Of aught achieved
Whereby his reign on earth might be believed;
Or his superb effrontery be conceived?

That he — of all God's creatures niggling-nice,
Yet seamed with pride, conceit, and racked with vice;
Dove-gentle; saintlike; evil as cockatrice —

Should thus have edged his way from clime to clime
In a mere millionth of terrestrial 'time',
And talked of Truth, of Wisdom, the Sublime!

Once, a bold venturer, perched on his *'Machine'*,
Broke out (Man's history over) on a scene
Of Sun stark still, and leprous sea brine-green.
And, for sole witness of life's Might-have-been,
A tentacled crustacean, vast, obscene!

'. . . But things to come exceed our human reach . . .'

Now — in a patch of sea-turf may arise
Low mounds secreting the packed enterprise
Of empires past all sapience to assize —
The latest of a myriad dynasties.

And when the heat of summer wells into
Their chambered queens, then their dark galleries through
Swarm they with their sheened courtiers up into the blue —

To glut the sea-gulls, or creep back to shed
Their cheating gnawed-off pinions; or, instead,
To blacken for miles the sea-sands with their dead . . .

Time? May God help us! Better a few years
Of casual change than slavery such as theirs:
Where all are pitiless, and none shed tears.

Once was a hidden country, travellers say,
(Due East-by-West of North-by-South it lay),
Designed to serve as a Utopia;
Where all things living lived the selfsame way.

Its flowers were scant and scentless (like our musk);
One weight of ivory was each tooth and tusk;
On every nut there swelled the same-sized husk;
Noonday to night there loomed perpetual dusk.

Fate was appalled. Her See-Saw would not stir.
Man sat dead-centre and grimaced at her.
Her prizes? None could shine where none could err;
So every artless dunce was a philosopher . . .

'. . . This infant world has taken long to make,
Nor hast Thou done with it, but mak'st it yet,
And wilt be working on when death has set
A new mound in some churchyard for my sake . . .'

Still in long clothes was I when learnèd men
Tracked down the 'atom'. They as busy had been
On evidences of a distant When
That mite had ape for kith and kin. Amen.

187

Once did the tiny shrews lemurs beget;
And they the tarsier, starred with eyes of jet;
And that the wistful little marmoset:
At length came Man; with Fate for martinet.
And *Time*? How could it else but aid, abet?

Still, there was other route. One no less free:
A virgin, visionary Earth to see,
Seed of supreme potentiality
Of man with God and love at peace to be.

Were life a poem we have to improvise
(Facing the stubbornest of all prosodies)
An Epilogue might close the enterprise;
And all else seem a mere parenthesis.
Which — when Earth's 'actual' thins — we know it is.

As when in pangs of death a hermit lay —
Cave, rill, rock, leaf-shagged tree — and from the sky,
Blue above sand, a seraph hovered nigh,

And set his foot there. Like a god's, his face
Shone in the shadow, smiling in its grace,
And shed infinity in that narrow space.

'The riddle nature could not prove
Was nothing else but secret love . . . .'

Cry on the dead: —'*Beseech thee! wake! Arise!*' . . .
Impassive waxen visage, fast-sealed eyes
Sunken past speculation or surmise:
And, for response, not even the least of sighs.

How, then, can he we knew and loved be *there*?
Whose every thought was courtesy; whose one care
To show his friendship, and to speak us fair:

Gentle and steadfast. Why, but three days since
We talked of life; its whither and its whence;
His face alert with age's innocence.
He smiled an *au revoir* when he went hence. . . .

Oh, ev'n should folly bring Man's world to woe,
Out of its ashes might a sweeter show.
And what of the life beyond, whereto we go?

Even were that of this a further lease
It yet might win to a blest state that is
Past thought — transcending scope of clock-time's bliss.
More simple, passionate, and profound than this.

'. . . "O Lord! methought what pain it was to drown!
What dreadful noise of water in mine ears!" . . .'

Dazed by mere 'Space' void-universes-wide,
Where All-that-is has Nought-that-thinks for bride,
The mind rebels. It's Reason's suicide. . . .

That dream I had of old — when, gazing sheer
Down verge of an abysm of stagnant air,
Senses as sharp as insect's, I could hear
Time's Ocean, sighing on the shingle there:

A whispering menace that chilled brain and blood;
Enormous, formless. Agonised I stood,
Tongueless with horror of what this forbode;

Yet lured on ever closer to its brim;
The night-long plunge; the gulf, vast, vaporous, dim;
That vault of Nothingness, the Nought of dream.

Ah, well I knew the doom in wait for me —
Lost in that quagmire of Sleep's treachery —
Drowning, to thirst for death; but never die. . . .

189

Yet never fiend that trod Earth's crust could break
Man's steadfast soul while he was ware and wake,
Though God Himself should seem him to forsake —
Unless, 'twould seem, such fiend took human shape.

And never in Matter, surely, shall we find
Aught that is wholly inconsonant with a Mind
That thus conceived, evoked, informed its kind?
Else to forlorn Unreason we are confined.

Why, then, so closely pry? Consider, too —
Despite the earth-bound lenses we look through —
At exquisite equipoise rests what is true;
'All knowledge is remembrance' . . . 'Nothing's new.'

Oh, with what joy an ignorant heart may steal
From dry-as-dust abstractions to a 'real',
Where what we think is blent with what we feel.

That star, which through the window spills its ray
On sheet and pillow when in dream we stray —
That's not a myriad light-years far away!

No further (if mere distance be at all),
Than is the ultramicroscopical —
The goddess who electrons has in thrall.

. . .What! 'island universes'! — thick as dew?
When even of huge Betelguese it's true
That distance lends enchantment to the view! . . .

Will ever indeed have tongue the power to tell
All ev'n a taper discloses in a well?
If Truth's it be, it's clean impossible.

Thick too as motes that in a sunbeam drift
Day's dreamlike images may swirl and shift
Too instantaneous for clock to sift.

Strive then to give them words. The wits fall numb;
Into a *cul-de-sac* thought seems to come;
A timeless semi-conscious vacuum.
And how long wait will they a lip that's dumb?

No more than stream till it is stayed in ice
Will with its waters glass the same scene twice
Can we recall Time's content as it flies.

Clear be its well-spring, then; its tide slow, deep.
Rich in reflection, let the quiet mind steep.
Peace comes but seldom, let not one crumb slip.

'. . . And all put on a gentle hue,
Hanging in the shadowy air
Like a picture rich and rare . . .'

Transient the loved may be. The ripple flows;
So is perfected — falls the wreathed musk-rose.
'Tis his own rainbow with earth's traveller goes.

One unique journey his. His dial tells
His own sun's passive shadow, nothing else;
Though nought its splendour, when it shines, excels.

And if in the familiar, prized, serene —
Green hill, and woodland, pool in twilight seen,
House we have loved, shared, treasured, talked, been happy in —
Our wonder and delight have always been,

Strange paradox it were, if it were true,
That, when the sight goes, then the see-er goes too.
What? For *that* finis a long life's ado?

Whence was that whispering — as if secretly?
A scarce-heard utterance, followed by a sigh : —
'*Some there may be who when they die, they die.*'
'*And their whole world goes with them ?*' came reply.

'*Why, it might chance he leaves some tale behind
Whose radiant aim had left him all but blind,
Which yet none living could for reader find.
So evanescent may prove all mankind :
Though ghost with ghost still commune ; mind with mind.*'

'*. . . Her rest shall not begin nor end, but be ;
And when she wakes she will not think it long . . .*'

Yet, even if, dying, we should cease to be,
However brief our mortal destiny,
Were this for having *lived* outrageous fee?

For having loved, laughed, talked, dreamed, toiled, endured
        our dree ;
    Ev'n cut *one* birthday-cake — with candles three?

That were to mere good sense clean contrary ;
As well might once-green skeleton leaf upbraid its
        Springtide tree.

Days there may come that wish there were no morrow,
No night of weeping, nor a dawn of sorrow ;
Yet only out of bonds as bleak and narrow,
Can we the rapture of forgiveness borrow.

Swift-falling flower, slowly fretting stone
Clock on unheeded those who lie alone,
Whose quiet dust in darkness may dream on
The more serenely if they peace have won —

And in earth's sempiternity awake
The annual yew-buds that above them break,
And to the winds their incense-pollen shake.

'... Sometimes Death, puffing at the doore,
Blows all the dust about the floore:
'But while he thinks to spoil the room, he sweeps ...'

Strange prodigy is Man. Of so short stay,
Yet linked with Vega and with Nineveh.
Time — Space: what matters it how far away,
In this strange Hall of Mirrors through which we stray?

Life's dearest mysteries lie near, not far.
The least explored are the familiar;
As, to a child, the twinkling of a star;
As, to ourselves, ourselves — who know not what we are!

Subtler than light, *Time* seems our eyes to steep
With beauty unearthly as things age; and slip
Into the timelessness Lethean of Sleep.

The Trumpet sounds. The listening arise;
Host beyond host the angelic hierarchies
Dome with their glory the once-empty skies. . . .

'An Old Wives' tale ...'? We smile; or yawn: refuse
Credence to fables which no more amuse
Wits braced and pregnant with the morning's News.

'Tale' if it be, 'twas by no idiot told
Of some far Golden Age to an Age of Gold,
Whose chief pursuit concerns the bought and sold.

Would you your cranium case of clockwork were?
Its mainspring cleverness, its parts all 'spare';
Its key mere habit, yet each tick, *Beware!*?

'... When yet I had not walkt above
A mile or two, from my first love ...'

Better than that, it were to stay the child
Before 'time' tamed you. When you both ran wild
And to heaven's *Angelus* were reconciled.

Host of all sun-blest things by nature his,
His mind imagines all on earth he sees,
His heart a honeycomb of far resemblances —
Ere fall the shadows, shams, obliquities.

The streams of air that throng his timeless sky
Toss the green tree-tops, and not even sigh

In the slim nid-nod grass that seeds near by,
Or rob by a note his blackbird's lullaby.
And when the day breathes cold, and winds are high,
To watch the autumnal jackdaws storm the sky ! —
Meal-dusty polls, glossed plumage, speedwell eye —
Ere cold of winter come ; and Spring draw nigh.

And though the beauty both of bird and song
May pass unheeded in the press and throng,
In its own small for-ever it lived long.

Not by mere age, renown, power, place, or pride
The heart makes measurement. Its quickening tide
Found once its egress in a wounded side :

Love is its joyful citadel. Its moat
A lake of lilies, though they wither not.
Beyond our plummet's reach lies where they float.

Yet may we sound that deep as best we can,
And, unlike dazed Narcissus, there may scan
Reflections of the inestimable in man :

All that of truth is in its mirror shown ;
And, far beneath, the ooze life feeds upon,
Whose *rot* breeds evil, jealousy and scorn.
A nature merciless, a mind forsworn.

'. . . He promised he'd bring me a basket of posies,
A garland of lilies, a garland of roses . . .'

> Love on; and faithfully. Death hath his pace.
> No past inveigles him. That timeless face
> Ev'n of the future shows no faintest trace;
>
> But what far-beckoning mysteries hide there,
> In those phantasmal sockets, bleak and bare?
> Visions frequent their dark; but not *Despair*.
>
> Mere fictions? . . . Still, how sweet upon your ear
> Was always, '*Once upon a time, my dear . . .*' —
> Robbing both night and morrow of all fear.
>
> Ev'n this enchantment soon as come was gone
> To swell that 'once'. And so you morrowed on.
> Is *that* why clocks set 'fast' you choose to con?
>
> Just to seduce the dotard with his glass
> By damming back his sands a while? Alas,
> A specious trick, poor soul! But — let it pass.
>
> Dog in the manger, Master Yea-and-Nay,
> You pine for time to hasten, yet bid it stay —
> Creature of contraries for ever at play.
>
> As seems the moon — when clouds in legion lie —
> 'Gainst the wild wind to race; till, suddenly,
> Her full effulgence floods a tranquil sky.
> And both are good — wind, and tranquillity —
> That vault of Silence, and the hoot-owl's cry.

Change lives not long, time fainteth and time mourns,
Solace and sorrow have their certain turns. . . .'

> And what worse fate were there than the decree: —
> '*Thy days shall pass in changeless impotency* —
> *Sand, salt, grey mist, stark rock and wash of sea* —
> *Thy one conundrum, How to cease to be?*'

Only the impotent grieve — '*The hours drag by.*'
Self is their burden. That's a bond-slave's cry.
Will it be *clock*-time, think you, when you die?
Or body's zero; soul's eternity?

Immeasurable aeons ere the sun
Sprayed out the planets, as a fish its spawn,
Clotho her fatal tissue had begun

Which lured you to this instant. And, know this:
Eve fell; the King looked up; cock crew; ywis
Woe, of a moment, was the traitor's kiss.

All in a moment Eros shoots, and flies;
Corroding hatred gazes from the eyes;
The heart is broken. And the loved one dies.

No wonder, then, that soon as day's begun,
Shadow foretells the course that it will run —
Cast by that radiant Prince of Time, the Sun;

Whom our dull clouds conceal; whom Earth forsakes,
And skulking denizens of the dark awakes.
It is her own withdrawal midnight makes.

'* . . . Man is the shuttle, to whose winding quest*
And passage through these looms
God ordered motion, but ordained no rest. . . .'

Journeying swiftly on, she makes no stay;
'A thousand years are but as yesterday':
By candle Alfred set his hour to pray:
And, once, Man merely Sunned his life away.

Now we devices have so accurate
They tell the exigent enquirer what
Sheer millionth of a second he is at —
Or *was*, if one must really get it pat.

Would they might pause instead!...
    Or slow, or fast,
Time's falling waters grieve,
    This cannot last!
In mere momentum merging with the Past.

Back to our homely hour-glass let us go.
It tells us nothing till we wish it to;
And, even then, in dosage smooth and slow. . . .

'... "O Time! thou must untangle this, not I." ...'

Ponder the problem how we may, and can,
Time has enigma been since Time began,
The subtlest of confusions known to Man;

One no less baffling than it is to say
How came what we call Consciousness our way;
Whence flows the wellspring that keeps life in play;
Or, this dilemma solved, where then 'twill stray.

Where Mind is not, there Time would cease to be,
All expectation, hope, and memory;
Without a warp how weave a tapestry?

Let there be Chaos! was the first decree;
And one of infinite potentiality.

Apart then from the whither and the whence —
What *is* this 'time' but term to mark our sense
Of life's erratic sequence of events,
Though not their scope and range or consequence;

And we its centre and circumference?

They fleet along, as if by Fancy led,
Like flotsam on a brook, and we its bed —
The world without; the mind-world, in our head —
Urgent, sweet, shattering; forlorn, half-dead.

Three score and ten . . . Like leaves our lives unfold;
Hid in the telling moves the tale untold.
It is not wishing makes the heart grow cold.
And saddest of all earth's clocks is Others growing old:
    The silvering hair that once was palest gold.

' . . . But most she loathed the hour
When the thick-moted sunbeam lay
Athwart the chambers, and the day
Was sloping toward his western bower. . . .'

Watched pots are loth to boil, old bodies prate;
Snail-slow moves *everything* for which we wait:
The craved-for news; the kiss; the loved-one, late;
The laggard footfall at the fast-locked gate;
Yes — and a dead man's shoes, if that's our bait.

All that we long for, languish, pray for — Oh,
Never moved Car of Juggernaut so slow.
It comes — and hours into mere moments flow:
For even on Innocents' Day the blade may show
Of Snowdrop piercing through the crudded snow
Snell though the starving blasts of winter blow.
        It's bidden, and wills it, so.

But drifts of living, eventless, feelingless,
Lapse out unmemoried into nothingness.
Instant and timeless are our ecstacies.

And should events be swift, wild, urgent — then
No cranny shows for clock-time to creep in;
Life leaps to action, even the sun unseen.

' . . . The mind, that Ocean where each kind
Does straight its own resemblance find;
Yet it creates, transcending these.
Far other Worlds, and other Seas . . .'

Not less remote that tick when one's engrossed
In arduous treasure-hunt on Fiction's coast,
Called El Dorado: with one's self for ghost.

Thus celled — aurelia in its cocoon —
In thrall of this strange make-believe, alone,
Phantoms appear, in seeming flesh and bone.
They breathe; live; move; they *are* — one's very own.
Scene, story and intent web softly on . . . .

You pause; look up: '*Good heavens; the morning's gone!*'

And as for Coleridge, spellbound with his *Rime* —
Whose music, radiance and strangeness seem
Real as the simulacra of a dream —

Four several 'times' he mingled in his theme: —
His clock's, his mind's, the ship's that had no name,
The Sun of genius', regnant over them. . . .
And *Kubla Khan* ?— when one from Porlock came?

' . . . Life is a Terrace-walke with an Arbour at one end, where we repose, and dream over
our past perambulations. . . . The Soule watcheth when wee sleepe. . . .'

Throughout the day throbs on this inward loom;
Though little heeded be its whirr and thrum.
Comes then the dark. And, senses lulled and numb,
The sleeper lies; defenceless, passive, mum.

Hypnos awaits him, and what dreams may come;
The Actual faint as rumour in a tomb.

Stealthy as snow, vicissitudes drift by —
Watched, without pause, by some strange inward eye —
Lovely; bizarre; inane; we know not why!
Nor what of Space and Time they occupy,
Who's their deviser, or whence his puppetry.

Once, dreamer dreamed (his candle just puffed out)
He'd travelled half earth's oceans round about,
Stormed-on, becalmed; wild chance-work and unsought;
To sea-wind's whine, surf's hiss, and dolphin's snort
Days, weeks, his ship had sailed from port to port;

Sweeping the tides for wonders she had run
A moon's five phases; whirlwind and typhoon;
Islands galore. . . .
                        At length, his voyaging done,
He woke — to find his wick still smouldering on!

Had he been gone two minutes, or — well, none?

He who in slumber deep doth lie
Is that far in eternity.
Near clock may strike; no heed pays he —
Time-less in his non-entity.

So may a drowning man his past descry;
Softly, yet softlier falls his lullaby.
And Lethe? . . . Much may hap twixt that last sip and sigh.

Head nods. Lids droop. What then may *not* befall
In realms where nothing's four-dimensional?
Where nothing's real, yet all seems natural;
And what seems ages is no time at all?

Even the Sycamore with her thousand keys
Could not force locks as intricate as these,
Nor Argus ravel out such mysteries.

'. . . Sweet Swan of Avon! what a sight it were
To see thee in our waters yet appear,
And make those flights upon the bankes of Thames,
That so did take Eliza *and our* James! *. . .'*

So, wake to sleep; and sleep to wake we stray;
And genius early treads the two-fold way: —

Sun in the willow trees, Avon's placid stream:
And there, a Child, caught up 'twixt wake and dream:

Learning, with words, two wonders to condense —
A marvellous music, and a matchless sense.

Say that this came of the air — what matter that?
Desert, or tarn? Rocks where the Sirens meet?
Between the stars? Or where the Nameless sit?
Or wrenched from adversity? — It's no less sweet.
It cannot be gotten for gold, nor is silver the price of it.

Ideas thus pent may like bright diamonds be,
Of a scarce-earthly diuturnity,
Their facets drenched with light's transparency
Of every hue we in the rainbow see:
Yet each gem single in its unity.

Alas, ev'n these too must
Of Wisdom itself be but the crystalline dust:
Their archetypes the Immortals have in trust.

'. . . O could my spirit wing
Hills over, where salt Ocean hath his fresh headspring! . . .

Friends have these ever been of Poetry's.
Unlike the plant called 'everlasting', this,
Never straw-dry, sapless, or sterile is;
And since its virtue in the simple lies,
The unlearned may share its essence with the wise.

Vision and reverie, fantasies, ecstacies,
No hours 'keep' they, when, ranging as they please,

Over the hills we fare . . . over the seas . . . .
Senses celestial, mind's antipodes,
Nought Reason can invoke, or Logic seize;
No chime but sea-bell's dallying in the breeze:
To where the sovereign Muses dwell — the *Hesperides*.

And any mortal whom They shall enchant
Their happy secret myrtle groves may haunt;
Nor Time, nor Age, nor Death the soul to daunt . . . .

'. . . *An Ecstacy is a kind of medium between waking and sleeping, as sleep is a kind of middle state between life and death . . .*'

But reef your sails upon the Sea called Dead:
Quicksands where *Ennui* skulks; and, visage dread,
Dumb *Accidie* awaits you, heavy as lead:
Salt-marsh, blind wilderness, and skies blood-red;
Your horologe a vulture overhead . . . .

When Dürer, rapt in *Melencolia* sat,
Did ladder, rainbow, the disconsolate,
The child no voice could rouse, no sleep could sate,
In that unfathomable silence prate
Of *time*? . . . Did bat squeak, 'Albrecht Dürer, it grows
    late!'?

Only the soul these symbols could portray —
That comet-stricken sea, those flames at play,
Midnight, bell, hound asleep; and — turned away —
That face, of woe and speechless grief the prey.
Timeless, in torpor of Despair are they.

'*Then it was Music that enchanted you?*'

Yet, while we gaze, a rapture is achieved,
As in the hush when music is conceived;

202

'Ah, yes, Sir. Music; which at times I hope I heard
(As if of water, instrument, or bird)
Echo in my 'poor rendering of the word.'

Its very beauty mourns it is bereaved :
Is grieved
The embrace that gave it birth can never be retrieved.

All things — by sorrow and truth thus tinctured even,
And so transfigured — this rare grace are given;
From life's poor temporal deceits are shriven . . . .

'. . . And Ruben wente out in the wheat harvest and found mandragoras in the felds . . .'

Even a drug may thus delude and cheat —
One word, 'assassin', is a proof of it.
Muffle your brain with hashish : and the beat
Of clock falls slow as echo in the night
In some primaeval cavern hidden from sight —
Stalactite whispering to stalagmite.

Hues as of Ishtar's Garden cheat the eye.
Into the distance slips the inert, near by ;
The far recedes into infinity.
And — if it listen — ear will magnify
The querk of cock to Roc's appalling cry.

Or dare those deserts where no zephyr stirs,
And coins gleam on, which age-gone travellers
Dropped from their camel-caravans. And theirs
The dog whose tracks have stayed unblurred for years.

Come sudden danger, dread, the soul stands still ;
An ice-cold vigilance freezes mind and will ;
And every pulse-beat seems immeasurable.

No less intent, as the doomed Russian said,
Are they who keep appointment with the dead,
And, their last journey, towards the scaffold tread.

'. . . Fancy, and I, last Evening walkt,
And, Amoret, of thee we talkt . . .'

But would you bid Time *hasten* — race?

Then sit
In fancy again with Chloe — once-loved chit;
By the clear stream, where may-fly used to flit,
The copse of hazel and the young green wheat —

That rose-pale cheek, loose hair, and eager tongue
Sooth as a willow-wren's the leaves among;
The silence as the water rippled along.

How feveredly you watched the shadows grow
Longer and darker in the deepening glow
Of sun to set so soon. So soon . . . . '*No, no!*
You shall not, cannot go!'

Drave the wheels heavily when last look and kiss
Left you forsaken of all earthly bliss?
A fleeting moment's paradise — then this?

The loved, the loving, idol or worshipper —
Which hated Time the most, as you sat there?
She, the so young, so heedless and so dear,
Or you who mourned her absence — she still near?

'. . . How could it be so fair, and you away ?
How could the Trees be beauteous, Flowers so gay ? . . .'

So Michael Drayton grieved; lorn, melancholy;
His mistress absent; her sweet company
Lost for a while, leaving him solitary: —

'Of every tedious hour you have made two,
All this long winter here, by missing you:
Minutes are months, and when the hour is past,
A year is ended since the clock struck last.'

' . . Did'st thou ever see a lark in a cage ? Such is the soul in the body . . .'

And so must once have felt the little maid,
Needling until the light began to fade,
My cross-stitch sampler-rhyme, so often read,
Words all but meaningless in her small tired head : —

> *Short is our longest stay of life ;*
> *And soon its prospect ends :*
> *Yet on that day's uncertain date*
> *Eternity depends.*

And what — his life's loved labour at an end —
Chose Robert Burton for farewell to send
His hypochondriac votaries? This, my friend : —

> 'When I go musing all alone,
> Thinking of divers things foreknown,
> When I build castles in the air,
> Void of sorrow and void of fear,
> Pleasing myself with phantasms sweet,
> Methinks the time runs very fleet.

> > All my joys to this are folly,
> > Naught so sweet as melancholy.

> 'When I lie waking all alone,
> Recounting what I have ill done,

> My thoughts on me then tyrannize,
> Fear and sorrow me surprise,
> Whether I tarry still or go,
> Methinks the time moves very slow.

> > All my griefs to this are jolly,
> > Naught so sad as melancholy . . . .'

'. . . Parvula . . . formica . . . haud ignara ac non incauta futuri . . .'

See that small bird — sand, water, groundsel, seed —
How tender seems its captor to its need.
Yet may its prisoned heart for freedom plead.

'. . . To effect the same exactly it is beyond the Arithmetic of any but God, himself. . . .'

As may one's own — this *Cage* that we are in —
Dangling in Time, though Time itself's unseen,
If the beyond-it is our true demesne,
Alike its tissue, and its origin.

Queer are its inmates. Though brief age they attain,
They cackle, argue, imprecate, complain —
As though some Moloch 'kept' them, for pure gain!

Whether we mope or warble, soon learn we
Mood, mind, and clock were ever at enmity.
What truth one tells the others falsify —
Prolong our griefs, give pleasure wings to fly.

If, then, Time Present goes so often awry,
Where seek the skill to judge the Future by? —

That void pretentious region where no time is,
Only incessant possibilities,

Haunting the sweet-sick half-expectancies,
Flowers of envy, desires and reveries
Which may fall sterile, or fruit quite contrariwise.

Yet — daring its vast vague uncertainty,
Defying chance, and blind fatality,
Man's noblest acts and works achieve did he.
All was 'imagined' ere it came to be;

That marvellous coral in Time's unstable sea: —
Wells, Ely, Fountains, Gloucester, Lincoln, Canterbury.

And on that verge — its echoing arch, its restless to and fro —
Two Worlds resort; the one called Dream and this — our weal and woe

But cheating mirage, too, when most serene,
  The Future's ever been —
An Ocean, as it were from cockboat seen;
With in-shore drifts of islets witching-green.

'Golden', or 'grim', or 'menacing' — in a trice
We paint the ineffable figment of its skies —
And are in Purgatory, or Paradise.

And every 'moment' we thus waste or spend,
Waiting on what we cannot comprehend,
Has it for sequel; and, no less, for end.

Day-dream, and night-, may richest pasture be —
There strays the Unicorn called Fantasy.
But why become so readily the prey —
Clean contrary to true sagacity —
Of spurious futures we shall never see?
How seldom foresight and the facts agree!

Plague on the blank forebodings, heart-ache, dole,
The grim chimæras which our wits cajole,
The signs and omens that never reach their goal;

The fears, the follies hung upon an '*If*'! . . .
Surely, of foes to peace, joy, love, belief,
Is not this Time Apocryphal the chief?

'. . . *She glode forth as an adder doth* . . .'

In mien how soused in guile. No hairspring *he*,
Buzzing brisk seconds busier than a bee.
He *glides*. . . . As stealthily and remorselessly
As did the Serpent to Eve's apple-tree.

'Time' sheened the splendour that was Absalom's hair;
Time stilled the Garden; seduced Judas there;
Sped the avenging blade for Robespierre;
Dogged Marx, in reverie drowned, through Bloomsbury
    Square.

Give Ruin room, Time cries, *my brother, Space!*
Whether Man win to glory or disgrace,
Things still corrupt, corrode, and leave no trace.

And with its aether-silent, deadening flood,
Which robs the unfolding flower of its bud,
Time cheats us of our loveliest for good.

All is in flux, the coming and the gone.
This massive globe rotates, zone on to zone;
5.59 at B at C's 6.1;
Its every sunrise leaves a day just done;
So, bland automaton, it circles on.

Cowed by the spectre which 'for no man waits',
Obsequious hireling of the witless Fates,
Time pins down ev'n Dictators to their 'dates'.

'You who never sate with your wings folded ....'

Still, *if* it's 'time' alone we hold in fee,
Why, load its every rift with ore, *pardie!*
At least be lively Ephemeridae.

Else, days may rot, like apples in the grass,
Sick worthless windfalls, once good fruit, alas,
Which even rootling pigs unheeded pass.

Now — with its whole penumbra, clear to dim,
Abject with misery or with bliss a-brim —
Is our Sun's universe, to its utmost rim.

'. . . Doth not our chiefest bliss then lie
Between thirst and Satiety,
In the midway ? . . .'

We know no other's 'now', though guess we may —
And in that guessing while our own away;
And 'nows' innumerable make up our 'day':

Beads, baubles, gems, strung close; and we the string;
Each one a reflex of the everything
Around it. As may rain-drop mirror Spring;
Or foxed old hand-glass, Winter, on the wing.

. . . And never was there myth in guise more ghast

And with each *Now* a rivulet runs to waste,
Unless we pause to stoop; to sip; to taste;
And muse on any reflex it may cast:

Than gluttonous Chronus, without pause or rest
Gorging his progeny to glut the Past . . .

Its source a region of mountains, east to west,
High snows, crag, valleys green, and sunken fens —
                    a region called the Past.

Elusive Memory's concealed demesne
Wherein all relics of the Once-has-been
In viewless treasury unchanged remain.
And yet a livelong novelty retain.
Breathe *Sesame!* and make it yours again.

With caution, lest ajar the door she set
Where lurks the half-conscious one had best forget.
Vast is her cellarage. Beware of it.
Only the winds of heaven can keep it sweet.

Ah, wastrel, Memory. Hear her laugh — or weep;
Casual, erratic; and how fond of sleep;
Life's league-wide cornfields — and one sickle, to reap!

Lift up thy face, thy guileless face, my child!
The grey beard wagged; the dim, bleached, blue eyes smiled:
I am the Past. And thou, Time undefiled.

There, for the while, may silent phantoms tread,
Vivid with light and life, though long since dead;
With whom we commune, yet not one word said. . . .

'. . . With "Hey my little bird, and ho my little bird,
And ho but I love thee dearly" . . . .'

I see a low square house. It's dusk. Within,
Half-crazed with dread as shades of night begin,
I stand in watch: and so for hours have been.

Behind me voices drone, where sit at tea
My guardians, mindless of my misery:
'A silly homesick child! All fiddlededee!'

Footsteps approach; pass by. And still not She.

Could she forget? Not care? Forbear to come?
Illness? Ev'n death? Alas. My heart falls numb.
Gone then for ever — mother, peace, and home . . . .

So, in a flash, my heaped-up years I span
To fill *this* Now, as, with uplifted pen,
I match that child with this scarce-changed old man;

Espy, as then, along its close-shorn edge
The longed-for bonnet top the hated hedge:
Anguish to joy — how brief that slender bridge.

'. . . In a valley of the restless mind
I sought in mountain and in mead . . .'

    Isles in oblivion such scenes remain;
    Poignant and vivid and passionate. And then
    Life's piecemeal picture-book shuts-to again.

    Oh, for pure attar, for one drop of TIME —
    Essence Hesperidean of morning-prime;
    How lustrously would it enrich this rhyme.

    What gem would it resemble? Brilliance? Hue?
    What, if — like *Ægypt's* pearl — dissolved in dew,
    It lay on the tongue, then swept the whole self through?

    But where's the Druggist with his Bottles three —
    'Time dead and gone', 'Time Now', 'Time soon to be,
    For use in any grave emergency?'
    What is his price *per* minim?
                             Search, and see!

'. . ."I do account the world a tedious theatre,
For I do play a part in't against my will." . . .'

    From London's swarm of clocks — Bow's to Big Ben —
    Our darting eyes extort 'the' time. And then,
    Back to the day's routine we turn again.

    In much that matters most whole centuries slow,
    Lashed to its creaking treadmill on we go;
    Its inmost purpose past our wits to know.

    Cribbed in by diaries, with their fume and fret;
    Chained to an almanac, lest we forget
    To tell the Moon when she must rise and set;

    Mock-solemn creatures, with our jackdaw airs,
    Our Loans, Exchanges, Markets, stocks and shares,
    And — squinting two-faced monsters — Bulls-and-Bears;
    Boredom and bankruptcy our recurrent cares;
    And Nobody, poor souls, to hear our prayers:

How *thus* win liberty? How thus to come,
With these poor fractions, to a sovereign sum?
Ensure ourselves our own continuum?
Dance with the stars in their choragium?

Ring the bells backwards! Ay, no pause; no ease!
There looms on high, the Sword of Damocles,
Dangling by the hair now hoar as Destiny's
Over the labyrinth of days, like these.

Tyrannies deadlier than of Syracuse
Slowly insidiously undermining us —
The heart's debasement, and the mind's misuse.

Man gone, his clocks gone, *Time* might fall asleep?
A halcyon brooding on the Pacific Deep;
That huge, slow swell — sans wrack or sign of ship —
Which from the heavens seems scarcely even to creep . . .

ONCE

'Les Chinois voient l'heure dans l'œil des chats.'

'*Once*', runs the tale, 'in the lost isle of Lyncke,
A Cat, long poised on Instinct's very brink,
Crossed it by chance: and found that she could think.

'No previous venture could her feat excel.
At one swift leap she'd borne away the bell;
Pouncing on notions past all count to tell,
Quick as a kitten with a ball of wool.

'High in her Monarch's kitchen, snug on shelf,
Half-hidd'n by ancient pots resembling Delf,
She'd sit, for hours, colloguing with herself.

'... Then gan she wondren more than before
A thousand fold, and down her eyen cast;
For never sith the time that she was bore,
To knowen thing desirèd she so fast ....'

'Motionless eyes upon the scene below —
Jars, bowls, pots, platters, dishes, stew-pans in a row;
All creature comforts man and feline know,

'Cream by the gallon, a ceaseless to and fro,
Copper, brass, crystal, silver, twinkling and a-glow,
Scullions a score, and Cook in cap of snow —
Her thoughts welled on. And all were apropos.

'Logic for Law, she ranged from A. to Z.,
Never deluding her now brass-bright head,
By speculation, or mere fancy led,

With chance-wise ray that might on it be shed
Had she roved off at N., Q., X., instead.

'She mused on Space and Time, on Mind and Brain;
The 'isms and 'ologies that to them pertain;
On Will, Fate, Fortune: then turned back again
To dredge what in her Unconscious might remain
And purged its sediment of the faintest stain ....

'She sniffed at ideologies — was sick;
Pondered on 'policy' and 'politic' —
Yawned, and enwreathed her chops with one long lick.

'Once, ev'n, ejecting a contemptuous look
Down on the Scene below, a vow she took
She'd some day learn these Humans how to cook.

'And so, alack, the years thus spent
Failed to benumb her with sublime content.
A mewling voice kept nagging vague dissent:
"What, now they're over, ma'am, precisely have they meant?
Are you the wiser for this banishment?" —

'And all those vats of choicest knowledge hers!
The mischief done by inward Whisperers! . . .
Dead-weary of her Past (the tale avers)
And even of the great philosophers,

'She supped: on tipsy-cake, to be precise;
Re-crossed her Rubicon; and, in a trice,
Resumed her sport of catching rats and mice:
Then slept; and dreamed; and slept. 'Twas paradise.

'. . . So in peace our task we ply,
Pangar Bán, my cat and I;
In our arts we find our bliss,
I have mine and he has his . . .'

'Then, winter come; and snow; and wassailing;
Crouched on the Jester's knee, she'd purr, (he'd sing),
Runes strange and secret upon Everything,
Gazing meanwhile intently at the King . . . .'

'Ah, had she learned to swim; to sail a boat;
Tread water — anything to keep afloat,
She might have reached the Mainland — though remote;
Been broken in to live by rule and rote;
Timed, taped, stampeded by the siren's hoot.

'No; old yet wise, and come to where she'd be,
Throughout Life IX all tranquilly lived she —
"Puss by Appointment to His Majesty".' . . .

'Nothing on Earth, no thing at all
Can be exempted from the thrall . . . .'
'. . . "And lest that I should sleep,
One plays continually upon a drum". . .'

'Breakfast at eight.' 'Adjourned till April 2.
'Au revoir.' 'No flowers.' 'Of a son.' 'Na-poo!' —
Thus Man clocks in, clocks out, his whole life through.

214

His Struldbrugg *Father Time* — starved, bald, and daft,
Must limned have been — scythe, hour-glass, fore and aft —
By him who blinded Eros; and then laughed.

Emblems like this were cuts on every page
In Abel's hornbook — Adam's heritage:
They'll serve, perhaps, until Man comes of age.

Meanwhile we grope — as might the withy-wind
Striving around the ecliptic to be entwined.
Clocks 'right', but differing, found us still resigned,
Till, seventy years ago, we changed our mind:
And Act of Parliament *the* 'time' defined.

'O sisters, too,
How may we do
For to preserve this day? ...'

Yet once, the kings being gone, as Scripture tells,
Heaven's host now silent, star-shine on the hills,
Came, with his coral and its silver bells,

To lull both Mother and Son to their first sleep —
Safe, for the while, in stable with the sheep,
Nor any carking Cross wherefore to weep —

None else but *Time* himself: once more a child;
The youngest of the Cherubs, and less wild;
Hawk paired with turtle-dove, and reconciled.

So still he sate, being both young and wise —
Poised on the verge 'twixt two eternities —
Beauty itself he seemed, in earthly guise;
And daybreak-blue the colour of his eyes ....

'Sing levy dew, sing levy dew, the water and the wine,
The seven bright gold wires and the bugles they do shine ....'

To me, one cracked old dial is most dear;
My boyhood's go-to-bed, its Chanticleer;
Whose tick, alas, no more enchants my ear.

Dumb on the wall it hangs, its hands at noon;
Its face as vacant as a full-blown moon;
The mainspring broken, and its wheels run down —

A kitchen chattel. No fit theme for rhyme;
That case encrusted with a century's grime.
And yet, it taught me 'how to tell the time'.

I knew a bank. . . . Ah, then was Time indeed.
Ere life's first buds had bloomed, and gone to seed —
And none unloved; least so, the lowliest weed.

Harebell, moss, pimpernel; a swift in flight;
The star of evening on the verge of night —
One's heart stood still for wonder and delight:

And in that pause to a far island came
Of strangest semblance, and without a name;
For ever changing, and yet still the same.

Flame was its beauty, and the sea its bliss;
Its every sound a secret music. Yes,
An island such as in *The Tempest* is —

Imaged in words, but Thulé of a mind,
Not only Shakespeare's, but of all mankind:
That which blest Poetry alone can find . . . .

'. . . *Motionless as a cloud the old Man stood* . . .'

'What *is* this Poetry,' self whispered self,
'But the endeavour, faithfully and well
As speech in language man-devisèd can,
To enshrine therein the inexpressible?

'See, now, the moon's declining crescent slim;
Thridding the stars in heaven she goes her way:
Yet doth she silver-tinge the virgin white
Of that clear cluster of jasmine on its spray.

'Ay, and my cheek her finger touched. I turned,
Through window scanned the seed-plot I could till,
And called a garden: and my heart stopped beating,
So marvellous its darkness, and so still . . . .'

'. . . "Long thou for love never so high,
My love is more than thine may be" . . .'

Ours is that wine; that water clear and cool;
That very vineyard; and the troubled pool;
Wherewith to fill the thirsting spirit full.

Our utmost reach is what their content seems;
What mind surmises, and the heart esteems —
Ev'n though it be as transient as our dreams.

The true, the guileless, meaningful, and fair
Rest for their essence on our heed and care;
These are Earth's everything, Heaven's everywhere,
However small the commons we ourselves may share . . . .

Index of First Lines